"Kathi Pelton's latest book *Finding Home* is like a huge hug from the Father. The pages are dripping with hope, the heartbeat of the Lord, and the Father's love. Kathi leads you through some of her personal seasons, and leads you into a place of hope and to your home in Him. God is establishing 'home' in this season in many ways and one of those ways is the awakening to the beautiful place of being 'at home in Him,' and I believe the Holy Spirit will minister deeply to you as you journey through these pages. Lean back into the arms of your Beloved and let Him pour His love afresh into you, refresh you, strengthen you, heal you, as the words He whispers 'I am your home' settle deeply into your heart."

LANA VAWSER, *Lana Vawser Ministries*, author, speaker, prophetic voice

"In *Finding Home*, Kathi Pelton has given us a powerful testimony to the goodness of God and his relentless intention to bring beauty into a life that otherwise might be nothing but ashes. She writes with unflinching honesty and raw vulnerability of her journey to find hope amid the anguish of walking through dark and dreadful valleys. Even there, she tells us, our Father's loving hand will guide us if we turn our gaze to him and let him wash us from our failure and despair. She proclaims with confidence that our wilderness journeys, our struggles and trials, always lead to a 'door of hope' (Hosea 2:14-15). I pray this book will bless you as you read Kathi's story of her journey from brokenness, to healing, to freedom in finding a place to rest in the glorious love and mercy of our God."

MIKE BICKLE, Director, *International House of Prayer Kansas City*

"I received a word from the Lord concerning coming home in this season: coming home to God, our authentic selves, and to family as well as church. About a month later I received this manuscript *Finding Home*. To come home we must know where home is — find it! God is HOME. What a powerful book. I found myself being unusually drawn in to Kathi's story. What revelation, what life! Simple yet profound. I couldn't set it down! Filled with reality, overflowing with hope. Authentic yet surreal. It's also a harvest book; one you can share with seekers. What more can I say? I love this book."

BARBARA YODER, Founding Lead Overseeing Apostle, *Shekinah Regional Apostolic Center*

"I've had the privilege of knowing Kathi Pelton for the last few years and can attest to the fact that she is a clear and pure prophetic voice. This book is an invaluable source of wisdom. Understanding what God is doing in the midst of difficult seasons and how to respond to him is one of the most important life lessons — especially for leaders. Kathi powerfully addresses this and much more. Your identity in Christ and understanding of his ways will be strengthened as you read this book. I highly recommend it!"

DAVID BRADSHAW, President and visionary, *Awaken the Dawn*

"The Father has promised to prepare a home for each of us in eternity. Our friend Kathi shares how He prepares it here for us on the earth. He loves to build our home and our lives at the same time! And as her pathway shows, the Lord meets us in every detail, through every trial. Candid and beautifully inspiring. You will find yourself drawn into the very heart of God in a way that changes you forever. You will love her journey! We did!"

JON & JOLENE HAMILL, *Lamplighter Ministries*, authors of *White House Watchmen, The Midnight Cry, Crown&Throne*

"My dear friend Kathi Pelton's book *Finding Home* is an intricately woven tapestry displaying the beauty and glory of the Father's love for his children. The understanding of our home being found in the arms of our loving Father, is something every Christian needs to encounter. Whether you have been saved for a short time or a long time, this book will touch the deep places of your heart, bringing you a fresh revelation of the Father's love. Now more than ever, it's time to come home."

DANEEN BOTTLER, *Ty and Daneen Bottler Ministries,* Senior Associate Leader, *Father's House City Ministries*

Mariah~

The door of hope (Jesus) is always open for you. He will always lead you home!

With Love~

Kathi Felton

2021

finding home

ALSO BY KATHI PELTON

30 Days to Breakthrough: Stepping into Peace
30 Days to Breakthrough: Becoming Bold and Courageous

(with Jeffrey Pelton)
The Yielding: A Lifestyle of Surrender
The Sounds of Christmas

(Contributor)
Prophet Sharing 2021

Inscribe Press
Creativity Unleashed

Hillsboro, OR

finding home

a doorway to hope

KATHI PELTON

Published 2021 by Inscribe Press, Hillsboro, OR 97124.
Printed in the United States of America.

Cover and interior artwork by Kathi Pelton.

ISBN 978-1-951611-28-6 (paperback)
     978-1-951611-25-5 (eBook)
LCCN 2021922175

This book is dedicated to my only brother Bob "Bobby" Cheli. You found your way home — and praised the One who loved you most all the way there.

Contents

Foreword

Finding Home.

There is so much implied in just those two words.

The word "home" could have very different meanings, memories or implications for you depending on your own experience or circumstances.

For myself, I think of my childhood home. And while there are particular houses that for seasons were also my "home," home was more about a loving family that lived in those houses. A place that I could come "home" to and escape what was often a rough and scary experience in the outside world, where I was bullied, experienced a lot of rejection, and often loneliness.

While I was still quite young, I met and married my amazing wife Jodie, we had our darling daughter Keely, and we formed a beautiful home of our own.

When I was around thirty years old, we were living in Perth, Western Australia. During that time my parents, who were still living in New Zealand where I grew up (a good seven-hour flight away) separated and eventually divorced. Divorce is always tough on children, but even as a thirty-year old man, with a family of my own, it was a painful thing to walk through.

One of the consequences of my parents divorce, and things that impacted me the most was the grief and sense of loss of "home." Of course Jodie, Keely, and I had our own beautiful home together, but living in a different country, away from family, I was somehow comforted that back in New Zealand, there was a place that we could still call "home," a place with my parents that, if all else failed, we could retreat/return to, for comfort, safety, love, a home-cooked meal.

My parents' divorce meant that that no longer existed. And even though they would now have their own separate homes that I was welcome in, it would never be the same. Of course, they are wonderful parents and this didn't change; I am simply referring to my heart's reaction to the loss of my home of origin.

It's actually part of the God-designed plan for our lives, that as men, we leave the home of our childhood, we leave our mother and father, are joined with our wife, becoming "one flesh" (Genesis 2:24), and create our own new home. This is God's design for us to have an earthly sense of home, but yet there still remains in all of us a desire for a different kind of home...

C.S. Lewis said: "If we find ourselves with a desire that nothing in this world can satisfy, the most probable explanation is that we were made for another world."

I would like to also suggest.... another "home." A home that can truly only be found in God.

In this compelling, insightful, and heart-warming book, my friend Kathi Pelton tells her own story, with great vulnerability, of her journey of "Finding Home." While like me,

Kathi has found her sense of home in her own family and being with people she loves, ultimately we are all searching for a place of belonging, a place of unconditional love and acceptance, a place that we just "fit." That place can truly only be found in intimate relationship with the one who created us, designed us, knew us before we were born, and knitted us together in our mother's womb.

Our true "home" can only be found in Jesus.

I pray that as you read through Kathi's amazing story, you too would "Find Home," just as Kathi and I have, and experience the tangible love, peace, and presence of God in a very real, fresh, and powerful way.

Be blessed as you read.

—BEN HUGHES
author of *When God Breaks In*, television host, revivalist, Founder *Pour It Out Ministries* (www.pouritout.org)

Introduction

I WAS GOING TO DO it again.

For seventeen years, wherever I lived, the bathroom was a place of safety, of purging my shame, a place of protection from the fear and utter confusion still battering my soul from my chaotic childhood. I had lived with physical and emotional turmoil in my home because my parents were going through their own pain and bitterness from marital affairs and divorce. My dad, out of his own tremendous pain, would sometimes unleash his frustration on me and it terrified me.

And, as a thirteen-year-old, I had been abused by a man who was invited into our home for a short stay.

So, as a way of escape, I would lock myself in my bathroom, where I felt safe until whatever storm was raging had passed.

Sometime during my teen years, I discovered that the shame and pain and despair that continually threatened to choke me could be somewhat alleviated when I threw up.

For seventeen years I was bound by bulimia. I could go into the bathroom, just as I did when I was a girl, lock the door, and find comfort and safety through purging.

I was a pastor's wife and a mom of four beautiful children.

I had family and friends who loved me dearly. I had gone through a great deal of healing and restoration from terrible depression, as you will read about in the pages of this book. And yet, I still fought with crippling shame and disgust, and when it would overwhelm me, I had to get rid of it.

This day, I walked into the bathroom to once again practice the act that would bring me temporary relief and a small sense of peace, false though it was.

And this day, everything was about to change.

My heart pounded and my hands shook, even as I anticipated the guilty, temporary relief. I walked into the bathroom and as I swung the door closed, I heard a kind and gentle voice.

"Daughter, will you leave the door open?"

I fell against the closed door, my face burning with shame. I was seeking to be hidden from everyone — even my heavenly Father. He could not come in and be part of this shameful act! For years, the bathroom door had been a barrier of safety for me. Somehow, I believed that not even my heavenly Father could come in and see what was happening. But now his voice was on the other side of the door asking me to open it and let him in.

I began sobbing. "No, God — please no!"

How could I let him in and let him see this terrible thing? Curled against the door, tears rolling off my chin, I continued to beg God to leave me alone, just for a short time.

Still, his presence persisted, patiently waiting for me.

Finally, reluctantly, I stood and opened the door. I hated letting him into this part of my life. Shivering and wiping my cheeks, I turned and knelt before the toilet to purge my shame. At that moment, I felt hands wrap around my hair and pull it back, away from my face. Then I heard a gentle voice.

"Kathi, from now on, I will always be here with you."

He had not come in to rebuke me or command me to stop what I was doing, but to reveal himself as a Father of unconditional love. He was not angry, merely tender and compassionate. As soon as I heard those words, I fell on the floor weeping. I could feel his comforting arms around me for the longest time, and I was set free from the filthy spewing of torment from the father of lies, and from the eating disorder that had ruled my life. If only I had opened the door and let him in years earlier! I had let myself be enslaved to lies that shrouded me in shame. I had allowed the fear that I would always wander in the wilderness of hopelessness, drenched in shame and regret, to keep me from the presence of my Father, who offered me deliverance and lovingkindness and genuine safety.

The depths of healing and love that poured over me that day in the bathroom, when I opened the door, still overwhelms me.

This is not a book about eating disorders, but I began with that story because it illustrates the message of the following pages: that even in the darkest wilderness of despair, our loving God walks with us and shows us a door of hope that leads us home. In the coming chapters you will read the story of my journey to find *home* in a world that always seeks to lead us astray and tempts us to build our own crooked structures. I share my story in the hope that you, who may find yourself in a lonely place, will be encouraged to look again for the door of hope to which even now God is leading you. By his grace, he continues to draw me into his heart where I truly find a place I can call home. He will do the same for you.

So, what do you think of when you see the word "home"?

Is it the place where you were born, nurtured, and loved? Or is it a vague and distant memory of shining hopes never truly fulfilled? Do you have a family gathering place, somewhere you can always return and be welcomed with a warm embrace; a foundation of love and security upon which you can always depend? Or is home just the place you go each day to flop down and escape the pressures of unending, stress-filled days?

Or tragically, does the word "home" represent bitter and fearful memories?

For many of my years growing up, home was often a place of anger and chaos, a cruel mockery of my childhood dreams of something beautiful, peaceful, and secure.

To truly have a "home" is meant to be an essential part of the earthly experience for every person ever created. Our Father God placed within each of us a longing for the love and nurture of a real home — a deep desire to be an essential part of a loving family. His intention is for us to experience that kind of beauty throughout our lives.

Yet, as we examine history we see the forces of hell continually warring against human flourishing; and there is no better strategy than to attempt to destroy homes and families. From the beginning, God has desired a family, and he created Adam and Eve to know the beauty and joy of his presence as the foundational center of their existence. When they replaced loving obedience and trust in the creator with a desire to "be equal with God," they shattered that foundation and disrupted the fabric of creation. Because of their foolish disobedience, they found themselves evicted from the home they had known and so greatly enjoyed.

Since that day, humans have been trying to find their way back. People strive and struggle to create their own kingdoms of security and peace, but without the Lord as the foundational center of their lives, they are building structures on sand. If only every man, woman, and child would understand that Jesus is our only true foundation, enabling us to stand amid life's trials and tribulations, earth would know the beauty of Eden and our lives would be fruitful and glorious, as they were designed to be.

Innate to every person through the ages of human history is the deep ache and plaintive longing for the beautiful home we have lost. In this book we will walk through the wonderful, and sometimes painful, wrestle to establish Christ fully as the foundation of our lives so we can finally find our way home.

I have walked with the Lord for four decades and with each passing year I find that I continually need the help of the Holy Spirit to align the foundation of my life with trust in my precious Savior as the Cornerstone. My journey to find home has been a metamorphosis of personal transformation and an ongoing discovery of what, where, and most importantly, *who* "home" really is. By God's grace, he continues to draw me into his heart where I truly find the place I can call home.

> *Unless the* LORD *builds the house,*
> *those who build it labor in vain.*
> *Psalm 127:1 (a)*

CHAPTER ONE

My Childhood Search for Home

*The more honest we are able to be about our lives, the
more healing and life we will know.
And healing, while it can be a longer process than
we'd hoped, is a grace-filled one that always brings joy.*
Staci Eldredge, *Defiant Joy*

ASK ANY CHILD WHAT HE or she wants to be when
they grow up, and most will respond with a ready answer: a
doctor, an astronaut, a fireman, a famous actor or musician.
Kids spend hours fantasizing the excitement of becoming
successful or rich or famous. They think that one day, they
will change the world.

When I was a little girl, I would have answered, "I just
want to have a family and a home."

I do not remember having even a single day of aspiration to a particular profession, or any dreams of being
famous so that people everywhere would know my name.
As a child, all I dreamed about was to one day have a loving
family, living together in a place I could truly call *home*.

Early years

I was born into an Italian-Catholic family that (in my early years) attended church every week, but I don't ever remember having anyone explain to me that God was real
and alive and that he loved me. Being a Catholic in a strong

Italian family was more like having a particular nationality than practicing a religious belief. To me, Italian and Catholic were one and the same! My mom taught catechism each week and a crucifix hung above my bedroom door; in my mind this was all part of being Catholic. Jesus was a statue; saints were colorful inhabitants of stained glass windows; and hard wooden pews were places to sit still and behave until mass was over.

An ever-changing flock of young priests were my parent's closest friends. Some of them even lived with us while awaiting a permanent position in a parish. I loved them and I loved the energy that these fun twenty-something-year-olds would bring into our home, but again, I don't ever remember hearing about God or how I could have a relationship with him.

What I do remember is the feeling that I would get when I read the children's Bible that my parents bought me one Christmas. I often found myself turning its pages because the pictures and stories felt like "home" to me. Years later, after my parents no longer attended church and their marriage was disintegrating, I still would pull out that children's Bible and find comfort in the stories within its pages. I do not remember if I believed the stories were true, but nevertheless, they felt safe and brought me peace.

Everyone in our family was Catholic except my Dad's great aunt, whom I had only met at my birth. No one in my family would associate with her, but she would occasionally send me boxes of Christian comic books and when I would hold them and read them, that same safe feeling would wrap itself around me. My parents told me to throw them out ("Your Great Aunt Lena is a crazy born-again Jesus freak!") but instead, I would hide them under my mattress and from time to time, when I could be alone, I would pull them out and read them. I had no idea what "born-again" meant, but I assumed that it must be a bad thing.

Over the years my dad and mom stopped attending church because we moved to a remote area in the Sierra Nevada mountains of California and there was not a church nearby. The longer they were away from church the more they joined social clubs and went to places where drinking, dancing and activity that hurt marriages occurred. Gradually, my dad became a functioning alcoholic, and my mom a functioning prescription drug addict. They were not your typical homeless drunks or street-hustling addicts; they were successful in their jobs and were always financially well-to-do. But behind the façade, their marriage and their family were falling apart. They were continually engaging in extra-marital affairs, viciously fighting, separating then getting back together, hiring and firing lawyers, and creating all kinds of chaos. Any semblance of genuine home was engulfed in the tornado swirling within the walls of our house, and my understanding of "family" was redefined by betrayals and division. Our neighbors heard the fights, and their friends saw the dysfunction. I sought comfort and safety elsewhere by staying the night with friends every weekend, and by age fourteen I began finding it in the arms of boys who could easily manipulate me. For a "price" I found temporary refuge in their arms.

During my high school years, I spent as much time away from our house as I could. One night, when I could not find anything else to do, I found out about a meeting at my high school led by a group called Campus Life. I thought that I would go merely for the sake of once again getting out of my house.

I quickly discovered that Campus Life was a religious group made up of kids my dad would have referred to as born-again Jesus freaks; just like my crazy Great Aunt Lena. I thought that I should probably stay clear of these people since my entire extended family had rejected and cut off relationship from my great aunt for her fanatical ways.

I would have slipped out of the meeting that night but there was no way to do it discreetly. Also, I had nowhere else to go and it was better than home. I was the type of young girl who could not say no to anyone; I was quite the people-pleaser. Therefore, I was stuck in this religious meeting for the entirety of the evening. At first I was cynical and bored, but as I listened to them share about Jesus and talk about their lives, that same feeling of home that I would get when I read my children's Bible or the religious comic books was flooding me once again. It felt so good, but I knew that it was not for me. I believed that our family was somehow inherently bad and that some people were inherently good but the two could not mix or be changed. I spent a lot of time observing people and when I would meet the families of those that I considered "good," their parents and siblings seemed to have the same goodness about them. The same was true of those who I observed as bad — the bad seeds came from bad families. This was my conclusion; I thought that this group must be a group of good seeds.

As I looked at the people around me, I wondered if the term "born again" was a hippie name for those who were awkward and unpopular but had found acceptance in religion. Yet, I could not deny that there was something different about them that I wished I had. They seemed to be genuinely happy. I never felt genuinely happy. I was always stiving to find attention or to be loved, even if the "love" offered to me was only a word to receive a desired result. As I listened to them talk, it was like the ugly sorrow of the world had not touched them. I, on the other hand, was saturated in the world and its cheap imitation of happiness. I knew that even if I was interested in being a part of these people, I could never fit into their group.

After the meeting was over, the leader, Daniel, sat with me in a quiet corner and began to talk to me about Jesus and how I could have a personal relationship with him. I honestly had no idea what he was talking about, but that warm sense of safety and peace — the feeling of "home" — once again flooded me. At the same time, I also wanted to run because I knew that I could never take part in the things he spoke of. But, because I was always a man pleaser, I agreed to pray a salvation prayer with him. As he prayed, I repeated what he said but knew that I was being dishonest, because I would never leave my life of boys, sex, drinking, and giving into whatever temptation came my way. It wasn't that I didn't want to live differently; I simply did not believe that I'd ever be able to say "no" to those temptations, or live without a relationship with a boy, which was the only acceptance I knew. I was so desperate for love and attention, and to find someone to belong to. I was looking for home and a place to call family, but I was looking in the only places I had been taught to look. I still had no real aspiration for success, education, or a career; I only wanted to be loved and to find home.

The next few years were increasingly ugly, as our family

life shattered. My mom carried on a five-year affair with a convicted felon in prison while my dad was bitter and angry, only becoming calm when he was drinking. My sister had become so angry that she often ran away from home, got into trouble, and attempted suicide. Her pain was played out in anger while mine was played out in passivity and shame. Home, instead of being a safe haven, felt chaotic and dangerous. I hated being there and resolved to spend my life finding temporary comforts, rather than believing in my false dream that true home could exist.

Occasionally, throughout those years, I would find temporary comfort in a Christian environment. I liked attending the Campus Life meetings, even though I knew I would never really be a part of the group. Daniel was still the leader and he had become persistent in his pursuit to save me. He was even able to persuade me into going on a weekend retreat at a Christian camp. I had spent weeks saying no and making every excuse I could come up with not to go, but one evening he finally cornered me and convinced me to say yes. I felt panicked about going with the group, leaving the familiarity of the world that I had created around me. But it was on the California coast (we lived in the California Sierra Nevada mountains) so at least, I thought, I can spend time on the beach. But I did not know what God had in store for me.

When we arrived at the retreat campus, we were all taken to the chapel where we were to be a part of a service before our first meal. I did not know anyone and was anxious. Everything was foreign to me — the culture, the people, and the atmosphere. When I walked into that chapel, I heard worship music for the first time in my life. All I had ever known before that evening were hymns in the Catholic church sung to the accompaniment of a loud pipe organ, and even that was a faint memory from my younger years. This was something different than I had ever heard. It was a sound that penetrated my hardened soul and pierced my heart with its beauty. I was not a crier but when the sound of the worship filled that little chapel I began to weep uncontrollably. It was like the sound of everything I had ever longed for. It was comfort and home and peace and warmth all at the same time. I did not understand what was happening to me, but I surely didn't want it to end. If I could have stayed in that chapel the rest of my life I would have done so; I had never felt such beauty and safety in my life. I longed with everything in me to be one of the people who were good so that I could be around this sound forever. I looked around that chapel at all the kids who were smiling with their hands raised to this God that I had never known, and I ached to have what they had.

One of the girls there took me under her wing that and prayed with me, spent hours talking to me, and she even bought me my own Bible and two Christian albums: one by Keith Green and the other by the Second Chapter of Acts. I soaked up her words and her prayers like rain falling on desert sand.

When the weekend was over, as I rode home on a bus, I remember sitting near a window near the back as tears poured uncontrollably down my face. I was sobbing because I had to leave this newly discovered atmosphere that welcomed me home. I had experienced what it must be like to be "good" and to feel pure. Maybe I had only been pretending, but those three days were like heaven for me. I had to return to the chaos in my family, to the demands of my boyfriend and 1 his expectations that came with keeping that relationship, and to my existence of finding temporary comforts to fill my aching heart. I was convinced that I would never again experience the love and comfort I had found those days by the ocean.

In the following weeks, Daniel told me about his church and said I would be welcome anytime, and I would occasionally sneak in and sit up in the balcony where no one could see me. I just wanted to hear the sound of worship and watch the people who had found a home in that place. Even if I could not be one of those people, I just wanted to sit in the midst of it and watch from afar.

New Life Begins

By the time I was seventeen, my dad and mom were engulfed in furious and bitter divorce proceedings. I was living with my dad, and one Saturday evening I looked out a window and saw him sitting on our deck, his face buried in his hands as he sobbed. My heart ached for him, so I went outside and sat next to him. Suddenly, I was so surprised at what began pouring out of my mouth. I told my dad about Jesus, about salvation, and about how connecting with Jesus felt like home. I told him about the sound of worship and how being born again meant coming alive through Jesus and inheriting eternal life. I invited him to come to church with me the next morning, and to my amazement he agreed.

The next day we walked into the building together and instead of sitting in the balcony, he insisted on getting as close to the front as he could. He was hungry and desperate to experience what I had told him about. During worship tears poured down his face, and at the end of his message, the pastor gave an altar call and my dad leaped to his feet and practically ran to the altar. I wept with joy as I watched my dad experience the love that I had felt on the retreat, although I didn't have the heart to tell him that I was not living for Jesus. It was not that I did not want to; I truly did not believe that I could.

The next week he tricked my mom into going to church. It was Wednesday evening, and he unexpectedly picked her up from the airport as she was returning from a business trip. She was not happy about this unannounced "pick up" from the man she was divorcing, and she was furious when he drove into the church parking lot. He told her about his salvation experience and pleaded with her to go inside with him and give it a chance. She finally, and reluctantly, agreed.

And just like my dad, after she heard the worship and the message, she was deeply moved and gave her heart to Jesus. She and my dad wept together at the altar as the Lord began to heal their hearts and their marriage. The following Sunday they renewed their vows with each other in front of the whole church. During their ceremony my thirteen-year-old brother gave his life to Jesus. A week later our whole family was baptized together, but I still had not told anyone that I hadn't committed my life to God! I was convinced that I could not change and was not strong enough to walk away from the lifestyle that had me captive.

My parents had fully given their hearts to Jesus and become faithful and energetic volunteers in the church. They still had healing and growing to go through, but they held nothing back. My dad was baptized in the Holy Spirit and delivered from alcoholism in the same moment. He read his Bible, prayed, and worshipped all time. My mom's change came a bit slower, but she was also fully committed.

Their excitement provoked them to want to see me fully come to Jesus, so my dad took me to the local Christian bookstore, and he bought me some Christian albums that I could play in my car. I honestly did not think that I'd ever listen to them but I loved that my dad did this for me. I threw them into my car with my secular tapes and forgot about them. One evening, I was driving home from work and reached down to find one of my secular music tapes and accidently grabbed the Keith Green tape that my dad had bought me. When the music came on, I was once again gripped by the sound that pierced my heart. I began weeping uncontrollably as the words washed over me. If my parents could be saved, was it possible that I too could be saved?

But as the months passed, I moved further away from any thought of serving Jesus since I had convinced myself that I just could not change or do what needed to be done. I became engaged to my longtime boyfriend and was preparing to graduate from high school. My parents had decided to move to a new location in California to get a fresh start, and I agreed to go with them and live there temporarily until my wedding.

The night before we moved, my fiancé and I met with the pastor who was to perform our ceremony. Jim seemed nervous and distracted, and I thought perhaps he was sad about me leaving for several months. As we chatted with the minister, he abruptly turned to me and said, "I have to tell you something."

He said that "God came into his room" the day before and told him he could not marry me. Jim had been raised in a Christian home, but he was not a believer. The experience shocked him and left him badly shaken, but he knew he could not ignore it. He said he resisted at first and tried to argue, but "someone or something" reached into his chest and pulled out his love for me.

He looked at me with eyes red with tears. "I can't marry you."

I was shocked. "Jim, please! What are you talking about?"

He looked at the floor and said, "I'm sorry. I just can't."

Heartbroken, sick with grief, I sobbed as I pleaded with him to change his mind, but Jim just shook his head and walked out of the room — and out of my life. I was trembling with sorrow, but inside me a deep and sudden resolve, unexplainable, unstoppable, began resonating like the sound of a gong. I looked at the pastor and with shaking voice told him that I was going to walk with God. He hugged me and told me he would be praying for me.

The next morning a large moving truck drove off from the house I had grown up in, taking all our possessions to a new home north of the San Francisco Bay Area. I drove alone in my car. I was heartbroken about losing the person that I loved and had planned to spend my life with, but I was also strangely excited and hopeful that this was the chance for me to start a new life. I was scared and reluctant and determined all at the same time. In twenty-four hours my entire life had changed course.

As I drove, absent-mindedly listening to the radio, I

suddenly heard a news announcer talking about a tragic small-plane crash in Texas that occurred that day, taking the life of gospel singer Keith Green and his two small children. I have no idea why a secular newscast was reporting the story, but the moment I heard the news I pulled off the road, weeping, and told Jesus, "No matter what happens in my life, I want to know you like Keith Green knew you. I surrender everything to you!"

God is able to cause all things to work together for good. Keith's tragic death became the open door for me to surrender and obtain salvation.

Pray this with me: "I let go of all belief that I am beyond hope, beyond help, or beyond the reach of the One who gave his all for me. I walk through the hope of grace that extends to even the 'least.' I receive the gift of grace and the hope of God doing for me what I cannot do for myself."

CHAPTER TWO

"You Complete Me"

So this is what it means to be a "new creation!"

My FIRST TWO YEARS OF walking with Jesus were like a dream come true. My entire life had changed, and I truly felt like the "old me" had died and a "new me" had been born. In his love and exceptional mercy, God surrounded my young life with beautiful believers, a wonderful new home, a church, amazing Christian friendships, a new city away from all the old familiar trappings and temptations, and so many desires fulfilled. His kindness and love took my breath away each day. I could not believe that I was a part of the family of God. It was as if the years of pain were suddenly replaced by hope and joy.

I would drive in my car with worship music or contemporary Christian music playing and cry with such joy to saved. I would often find myself stopping and looking around at my life with awe because everything around me was miraculous. There was not a single area of my life that had not been radically changed and it was better than any dream I had ever dreamed. I remember often saying to myself, *"God cheated for me!"* It was like he provided all the answers, even to questions that I did not know to ask and prayers that I did not know to pray for. I was experiencing a redeemed life that I did not deserve, but had been given freely just through saying "yes" to him becoming my savior.

During that first year I met Jeffrey, the man who would be my husband. He was twenty-four years old, loved God with all his heart, and loved me with no ulterior motives or impure conditions. He knew that I was a new believer, and he took my hand to walk me deeper into knowing God and experiencing what a godly relationship looks like. Our time dating was so beautiful, and he was so honoring of me. He did not let my past become a stumbling block for our new love but received me as the daughter God had made me to be. My life was suddenly surrounded by beauty. That September, I walked down the aisle to be joined in marriage to a man that far exceeded any dream I ever had. Worship music filled our ceremony and after he kissed me as his bride, we walked back down the aisle together to the first worship song I had ever heard, "The Easter Song" — which is about being born again!

During our wedding reception we had a receiving line, where the bride and groom, their families, and the wedding party line up, and greet the guests and thank them for coming. At one point, I noticed two women in line that I did not recognize. One was an elderly woman, and she was leaning heavily for support on the arm of a woman about my parents' age. I asked my new husband if they were a part of his family and he replied that he had no idea who they were. When they finally came to Jeff and me, the elderly, frail older woman looked me in the eyes while taking my hands and said,

"I am your Great Aunt Lena and I have been praying for you since the day you were born. I came today to see the fulfillment of my prayers."

The only time this beautiful woman had ever seen me before my wedding day was the day I was born, and yet she had prayed for me throughout my years of pain and searching. She had no knowledge of what I had been through. We had not told her of my salvation or my marriage, but there she was because the Lord had revealed it to her. She looked at my born-again dad and mom and they embraced her and received her with tears of joy. She looked at my born-again little brother and she looked into my eyes, and she drank in the fulfillment of her prayers for our salvation and for her to be received back into the family. In this receiving line she was received, and she also received the joy of prayers answered. She came, she looked into my eyes, and then she left and soon after went to be with Jesus. She had taken my hand through prayer and led me home.

There is a scene from a movie where a deaf couple is in an elevator and the young man uses sign language to say to his beloved, "You complete me." That is what I want my life to say when Jesus looks into my eyes: "Jesus, you complete me." Only God could answer the prayers of a woman who poured her heart out for a family that had completely rejected and mocked her. Only God could hear the desperate cry of my heart to be able to walk with him and live in the refuge of the sound I heard when I was fourteen years old in that little chapel by the beach. Only God could reach in and set me free from an engagement to someone who would have led me down a road of separation from him. And only God could orchestrate the details and events that would have to occur to save my family and to move me to a place a new city where his hand had set up a future and a hope for me — and a family and home. His love made a way where there was no way.

My story stands for everyone's story. We see that God's kindness, mercy, and overwhelming grace rode on the prayers of a saint and transformed the life of a young girl who was looking for home.

CHAPTER THREE

Home Begins in the Wilderness

"If you get lost, stay still and I will find you."

HAVE YOU EVER GONE FOR a long walk or a drive in an unfamiliar place, and suddenly realized you were lost? Most of us never venture far without some form of guidance, especially in these days of online maps and directions on our ever-present cell phones. But if we were to suddenly find ourselves alone, far from any comforts of civilization, cut off from familiar securities and resources, surrounded only by wild woods and animals, we would feel vulnerable and frightened. Hacking through thick underbrush, plunging through rushing rivers, or scrambling to the top of a rugged mountain peak are certainly not the experiences we dream about when we reflect on the warm comforts of home and family.

Yet, throughout Scripture, we see the heart of God continually working with his people, leading them (and us) patiently, relentlessly, toward the blessings of his presence dwelling with us. Often we must wander through "dry and thirsty lands" before we discover that our restless hearts only find peace when we find our home in him.

Home is wherever the Lord is! But sometimes, like the prodigal son, we journey to "a distant land" and then find ourselves in trouble.

I remember when I was twenty years old, my husband and I had just moved to Baton Rouge, Louisiana, where he was attending college, and I needed to go grocery shopping after a long day at work. It was dark and I did not know my way around the city (this was in the days before cell phones or GPS). I had gone to an unfamiliar area of the city that was still mainly unfamiliar to me to shop, confident that I could easily return the same route I took to get there. When I was done with groceries safely loaded in my car, I drove out of the parking lot and promptly took a wrong turn, causing me to head in the wrong direction. Suddenly was I was completely lost. I did not have any coins for a pay phone and honestly did not know who I would call anyway, since Jeff was at a night class and I did not know anyone in the area.

As I drove, looking for anything even remotely familiar, I began to panic. Will I ever find my way home? I had driven out from the city limits, and could not even remember how to find my way back to a populated area. I had gotten off the "beaten path," and there were many dark, foreboding bayou sections away from the city lights. I was lost and scared. After over two hours of frantic driving, I finally found a familiar landmark and worked my way back to the college. I pulled into a parking lot, got out of the car, and walked to where I knew I would find my young husband and when I saw him, I just fell into his embrace, weeping. I had found home in his arms.

The year 2021 began a bit like this for me. It felt like walking out onto a favorite and familiar path, but then somehow taking a wrong turn into unfamiliar wilderness with no path, no way to communicate, no sense of direction — alone, cut off from warmth and security. Honestly, I was disoriented and felt a bit of that old "panic" that I had experienced as a twenty-year-old in a strange city. I just wanted to find my way home to what was familiar again.

The five years previously had been rich and full of God's tangible presence. Jeff and I were traveling to speak and to pray throughout the nations, and we were experiencing the blessing of connection with the beautiful family of God every place we went. For many years we had focused much time and energy on blessing nations other than our own United States, but in January 2020, the Lord moved us from the West Coast to the Washington D.C. region to be part of a number of prayer and ministry initiatives taking place. We were so excited about this new assignment and new experiences, believing we would see our nation, return to the place of "In God We Trust."

Within two months of our move COVID-19 hit our world and everything changed. Yet, since it was an election year, our move to Washington D.C. merely gave us more opportunity to be a part of prayer, worship, and strategic initiatives for our government. We felt like we were running with the wind at our back and his banner of love over our heads.

When the 2020 elections introduced greater turmoil in our nation, we felt it keenly in Washington D.C. It seemed like hitting a wall at full speed. We continued to put our hope in the Lord and in what He had called us to do but our hearts were troubled, and joy had suddenly turned to weeping. Then, on December 31, I received a phone call from my younger brother and his wife asking for prayer, because he had contracted COVID-19 and was taking a turn for the worse. Our family gathered around my phone and prayed for him before his wife drove him to the emergency room, where he was admitted and she was told to go home, as the hospital would not allow family members to be in the room with him. Over the next twenty-one days we fought for his life day and night in prayer. He could send text messages but was too short of breath to talk to any of us. Bob had battled lymphoma in the previous years but had overcome and been declared cancer-free in 2020, and at fifty-three had been in great health, until he contracted the virus.

On January 21 my brother drew his final breath. Grief pummeled me the first month of 2021 like a punch in the gut. My brother was a pastor and missionary to Honduras and yet all our prayers did not save him. We had been praying continually for a return to righteous standards for the United States, yet with the election results and the anger and violence taking place, those prayers also had seemingly not prevailed. My heart was filled with sorrow.

As February began, I tried to find something familiar spiritually and emotionally that would lead me back to the path that I had known — the path home. I felt lost and everything seemed dark. Each day was filled with varying degrees of numbness, grief, longing, surrender, and weeping. Nights were the worst because even the beautiful "God dreams" that had accompanied my sleep for many years had ceased and my nights were filled with bad dreams. I would wake up each morning even more disoriented than the day before.

Finally, one morning as I prayed, felt that I heard the words parents often tell their young children if they are somewhere away from home:

"If you get lost, stay still and I will find you."

My eyes filled with tears. I had struggled so hard in my attempts to make my way back to my Father's side, but I only succeeded in tangling myself in a web of sorrow and loneliness. So, I stopped trying to find my way home — the way back to intimacy and the "home" I had known with Jesus.

I had to cease striving and get very still. I needed to wait for my Father to find me where I was.

Instead, I have calmed and quieted myself, like a
weaned child who no longer cries for its mother's milk.
Yes, like a weaned child is my soul within me.
Psalm 131:2

I stopped long enough to remind myself that God has never left me or forsaken me. I stopped looking for a way out of the wilderness and began waiting to find him in the wilderness. I stopped so I could learn once again to "calm and quiet my soul" in his arms of faithful love.

I had to again become that twenty-year-old who found home in the arms of her young husband after getting lost in a strange place.

Can we find your home even in an unfamiliar and strange place where there is weeping? I believe that we can. We can find refuge in our Lord's everlasting arms even when our souls cannot comprehend or understand the world around us. In the wilderness we can rediscover that he is everything that we need.

The opening verse of Psalm 131 says,

LORD, my heart is not proud; my eyes are not haughty.
I do not concern myself with matters too great or too
awesome for me to grasp.

I believe that there are times that we begin to concern ourselves with matters too great and too awesome for us to grasp. They begin to become a "master" over our lives, and we try to figure out how to do what only God can do. It is in the times that we suddenly find ourselves in a wilderness that we must humble ourselves and once again become like a child. It is then that we must become still and remember that he is God.

He says, "Be still, and know that I am God; I will be exalted
among the nations, I will be exalted in the earth."
Psalm 46:10

As I already wrote, I walk with believers in other nations (many of which are now facing persecution) and it has been a tremendous blessing as well as powerfully humbling, but as 2021 emerged, the matters concerning other nations had become too great for me to grasp while dealing with the death of my brother from Covid. The matter of life and death was too awesome for me to fully comprehend and so God brought me into a wilderness place to restore me to "home."

Therefore, I am now going to allure her; I will lead her
into the wilderness and speak tenderly to her. There
I will give her back her vineyards, and will make the
Valley of Achor (Valley of Trouble) a door of hope.
There she will respond as in the days of her youth, as
in the day she came up out of Egypt. "In that day,"
declares the LORD, *"you will call me 'my husband'; you*
will no longer call me 'my master.'"
Hosea 2:14-16

The wilderness does not feel good but as I have discovered a few other times in my life — this "Valley of Trouble" is usually a door of hope that restores my soul and ushers me into a place of greater abundance.

…out of [the wilderness] came the message of my life,
or at least, the beginnings of it. And now I am able to
know from my own life — not somebody else's — who
God really is.[1]

No one asks for a wilderness season but when we suddenly find ourselves there, we must embrace it rather than thrash against it. It is in the secret and dark valleys that we must pull on the strength given to us in the mountaintop seasons. Often our first response to the unfamiliar wilderness is to begin running frantically, but that only serves to get us more lost. This is where we must stop, get still, and know that he is God. He is with us in the wilderness, and he will feed us, hold us, restore us, and deliver us in every area that you have become enslaved to false "masters." This is where you find him as husband. This is where you run into his arms and find him as home. Then, you will hear,

Who is that coming up from the wilderness, leaning on
her beloved?
Song of Solomon 8:5

I think that all too often we take on things that are too great for us to grasp and they enslave us under a weight and burden that becomes a harsh master over us. We must realize that when we have done all we can do, it is time to get still and stand (Ephesians 6:13). Stand in the confidence of who the LORD is; stand in the arms of the One who created all. The earth is his and all that is within it. Our partnership with him is within the beauty of a "bridal covenant." We are no longer in a "slave and master" relationship. The power of

---

1   Ken Gire, *Windows of the Soul* (Grand Rapids, MI:- Zondervan, 1996), 106.

covenant is where the enemy of our souls loses his footing and love wins.

Isn't it time to stop running, stop striving, stop panicking? Home is with you — right where you are. He is always with you, so be still and let him hold you until you are fully restored, leaning on your Beloved! Throughout the chapters of this book, we will explore and discover home together. We will find the door of hope that leads us home, even as we traverse the Valley of Trouble; and we will seek to see the names of unrighteous "masters" broken from our lives so that we come up out of the wilderness to fully lean upon our Beloved, whom we call Husband. The wilderness can be a hard journey, but it will be the most redemptive journey we ever take, and we find that the way through wilderness is the path to the rich warmth and beauty of home. Let us begin to search for that door of hope.

CHAPTER FOUR

First things First

*To bypass the wilderness in our journey to the
Promised Land is to bypass God. And what is the
use of occupying a land of promise unless the God of
promise goes with us?*
Jamie Buckingham, *A Way Through
the Wilderness*

EVERY TIME I HAVE FOUND myself in the wilderness,
I have been caught off guard. It is interesting that when
we are about to camp or backpack in the wilderness, we
spend a great deal of time preparing. The tools and gear
we need are quite different than the resources we gather
around us to live in our homes. Yet, when I find myself
traveling through a wilderness of the soul, I feel completely
unprepared and ill-equipped for the journey. I feel vulnerable, exposed, hungry, and completely lost. I must remember
that the Spirit of God within me has all the tools I need to
survive, even thrive, in these wilderness seasons. It is a "by
My Spirit" time; not a "might and power" time.

Each time that I find myself in this place, I have come
to learn that my wilderness "wanderings" are places God
has "allured" me to.

The Hebrew word translated "allure" is *pâthâh* which
can mean persuade, induce, or entice.[1] With that in mind,

---

1   "Pâthâh," *Key Word Study Bible* (Chattanooga, TN: AMG
Publishers, 2015), 2171.

look again at Hosea 2:

> "Therefore I am now going to allure her;
> I will lead her into the wilderness
> and speak tenderly to her.
> There I will give her back her vineyards,
> and will make the Valley of Achor a door of hope.
> There she will respond as in the days of her youth,
> as in the day she came up out of Egypt.
> "In that day," declares the Lord,
> "you will call me 'my husband';
> you will no longer call me 'my master.'
> I will remove the names of the Baals from her lips;
> no longer will their names be invoked.
> In that day I will make a covenant for them
> with the beasts of the field, the birds in the sky
> and the creatures that move along the ground.
> Bow and sword and battle
> I will abolish from the land,
> so that all may lie down in safety.
> I will betroth you to me forever;
> I will betroth you in righteousness and justice,
> in love and compassion.
> I will betroth you in faithfulness,
> and you will acknowledge the Lord.
>
> "In that day I will respond,"
> declares the LORD—
> "I will respond to the skies,
> and they will respond to the earth;
> and the earth will respond to the grain,
> the new wine and the olive oil,
> and they will respond to Jezreel.

I will plant her for myself in the land;
I will show my love to the one I called 'Not my loved
one. I will say to those called 'Not my people,'
'You are my people';
and they will say, 'You are my God.'"

God was speaking to Israel after the Assyrian invasion and judgment on the land. God's *alluring of her* was a call to repentance, to restoration, and to an outpouring of his extravagant love.

Sometimes the Lord also *allures* us to the wilderness after a long and busy season, even a fruitful season, to be pruned and to rest, and to be restored to our *first love.*

We are always growing as we journey with the Holy Spirit. Often in the process we can find ourselves unconsciously serving the "master" of ministry or the opinions and approval of others more than simply walking hand-in-hand with our Beloved. Just as in marriage, if we do not take time to get away with our spouse from the responsibilities, the crowds, the busyness of life, then our marriage relationship will become bound by the things we are responsible for and the things that we do, more than a deep connection with each other. How many married couples have you heard say that they stayed together because of their children or the house or business that they own together? Would it not have been better for them to nurture love and covenant than enslave their lives to the masters of this world?

Obviously, we need to pour into our children and steward the responsibilities the Lord has placed before us, but not at the expense or neglect of intimacy. So God, in his lovingkindness, will allure us away from the chaos and draw us into the place where we rediscover the pure joy of first love. First love with Jesus is the shining manifestation of that statement, "You complete me." And being in the grip of the completeness of first love is truly the home that we all long for and were created for.

At first, finding ourselves in the wilderness is usually shocking and disorienting. We usually do not experience spiritual clarity and understanding, where our spirit says to our soul, "This is good." Instead, we normally will react and seek any means to find an escape and make our way back to our safe, controlled, "city dwelling." An initial sense of panic is common as we enter the *Valley of Achor* (Trouble). How many of us would stop on a mountaintop and ask for a threshold to the Valley of Achor to open before us? Yet God, in his kindness and his amazing grace, mercy, and wisdom, ushers us into this place where we receive a reset and personal reformation.

Isaiah 40 talks about *clearing a path in the wilderness* so that the glory of the Lord will be revealed. I have found that each time I have been in a wilderness season that I have come out of that season with more of my life cleared and leveled so that the glory of the Lord is able to be revealed through me.

> *A voice is calling, "Clear the way for the LORD in the*
> *wilderness;*
> *Make smooth in the desert a highway for our God.*
> *"Let every valley be lifted up, And every mountain and*
> *hill be made low;*
> *And let the rough ground become a plain, And the*
> *rugged terrain a broad valley;*
> *Then the glory of the LORD will be revealed, And all*
> *flesh will see it together;*
> *For the mouth of the LORD has spoken."*

This is my prayer during the times that I have found myself in the wilderness — that a way will be cleared for his glory to be revealed in my heart and life. That every place that has been lifted higher than him will be brought low and every place that has become rough and rugged will be made smooth with broadened room for his glory.

As humans, we need pruning and purifying from time to time. Our self-sufficient attitudes subtly exalt themselves above trust in our God, and replace walking in full dependence upon him with thinking we can make our own way. I personally can become extremely comfortable in extended times of blessings and fruitfulness. Though we want to be a tree planted by the river of God that yields fruit in every season, to be more fruitful than in previous seasons we must go through times of pruning. I believe many in the body of Christ entered a time of pruning and purifying as we moved into 2020. We need to keep in mind that if we will draw near to the Father and allow him to prune us, he makes a way for his glory to be revealed. Although the process of pruning is painful and difficult, it helps to remember that he has already given us his glory, but there are "branches" growing in our lives that must be pruned — areas within us that prevent his glory from being fully revealed. Do not worry; you will not miss anything during your time in the wilderness if you will yield to his precise pruning.

In the following chapter I share one of my first wilderness seasons. There is a lot to be learned when we spend extended times there. Each person will have different experiences, emotional responses, and postures during these times, but we can learn so much from those who have gone before us. I have discovered in these times that the road through the wilderness has always ushered me closer to finding home than any other journeys I have taken.

The Door of Hope

Do you know that Jesus is interceding for you? There has never been a moment of your life that his intercession has not been going forth for you, and his heart has not been filled with longing for intimate fellowship with you. He continually reaches out to you, and will do whatever is necessary to draw you into life with him that will cause you to flourish. Open the door that leads you to the answers to his intercession — it stands before you now and is full of desires fulfilled and unceasing joy.

CHAPTER FIVE

My Dark Night of the Soul

*On this earth, then, in our deserts, God personally
reveals and names himself. When he does so, his
pleasure floods our senses, his beauty engulfs us...The
knowledge of who he is and the never-ending implications of being his children overwhelm us.*
Marlena Graves, *A Beautiful Disaster*

AFTER THE BIRTH OF MY fourth child, I found myself spiraling into a darkness and depression that I did not
know was possible to experience. During the second tri-
mester of my pregnancy, I was diagnosed with preeclampsia — a complication causing high blood pressure, signaling
damage to other organ systems; most often the liver and
kidneys. By my seventh month the doctors were no longer
able to control my condition and decided to induce labor.

My labor was traumatic for everyone involved, including my doctor and labor nurse. Both my baby son and I
nearly died. The doctors had to resuscitate my baby while
he was still in my womb. I was later told that the hospital's labor department was forced to use every machine
they had during my labor, since my life and my baby's life
were in peril. The day after his birth my condition was still
extremely serious. That night, lying awake in my hospital
bed, I saw an inky black, dreadful figure enter my room. A

stench of death permeated the atmosphere of my room, and I was terrified I was dying. The shriek of alarms from the machines I was hooked up to began sounding, and the shadow left, leaving me shaken and even more exhausted. I do not know if I saw something real or if I hallucinated due to all the medications I was being given. Either way, I felt certain a spirit of death intended to take my life. I begged the nurse to call my husband to come and be with me because I was so afraid and in so much pain. Jeff came and prayed for me, sat with me and assured me that we would be okay.

When my son and I were healthy enough to return home, I noticed anxiety and sadness were hard to shake; they seemed to be increasing rather than decreasing. I adored my precious son, but something did not seem right within my body and soul. I had postpartum preeclampsia, requiring ongoing observation and medication for high blood pressure, but I did not attribute my struggle with anxiety or sadness to having just given birth. I now believe that my pregnancy and complications had triggered the onset of postpartum depression. Had I realized this, I may have been able to get medical help early on.

Jeff and I were on the pastoral staff at our local church, so I kept busy with ministry, friends, and my four kids to keep the depression at bay. But one day when my son was almost a year old, it was as if the floor disappeared under me and I began falling into a dark pit with no bottom. It was so excruciating that every moment of every day it was difficult to even breathe. I felt continually as though I had had the wind knocked out of me. I cried constantly and the pain from my childhood engulfed me, fresh as if I was reliving it. I did not know what was happening to me and seemed to have no control over it. I felt like I was in a vehicle with no brakes on a downward slope, speeding out of control.

I had always considered myself a happy person who overcame adversity, who viewed the world through the filter of a "glass half full" rather than "half empty." I had experienced sadness and mild depression while going through years of infertility, but this was something altogether unfamiliar and unimaginable. I often could not have a conversation and felt emotionally cut off from those around me due to the severity of my pain and despair. I started seeing a Christian counselor but that seemed to only make matters worse. The more we talked about my painful childhood, the worse it became. I honestly wished that I had never brought it up. On top of everything else crashing in on me, I was aware that I needed to deal with the addiction to bulimia that had consumed my life for years.

After more than a year of non-stop, severe depression, and realization that I was on a course headed for destruction, I entered a sixty-day treatment center for eating disorders. I was a pastor's wife and the mom of four young children; I had a beautiful home and a supportive, loving husband; but I fought suicidal thoughts every day because my pain was intolerable. I was not able to find comfort or peace no matter what I did. I was not merely in a wilderness; I was certain I had been flung into a grave and buried alive. Yet I continued living, with no respite from relentless agony. I did not understand where this came from or why God was not setting me free. Although I had found salvation at the cross when I was eighteen years old, I had not allowed the pain that I had experienced prior to that time to be healed. I ignored the trauma of the past and took on my new identity. But the depression that had been triggered by my pregnancy was evidence of wounds much deeper and darker than I wanted to admit.

At the treatment center, I learned a great deal about eating disorders and received tools to help me cope in a healthy fashion. But even armed with such understanding, after I returned home I sank deeper into depression. Eventually I resumed my addiction to bulimia, once again hiding it from everyone who cared about me. It seemed my feelings of wretchedness had only increased.

Into the Darkness

Finally, about two years later, in a moment of despair, I tried to take my life in the middle of the night by swallowing a huge handful of pills. I honestly believed that my family would be better off without me since I was beginning to believe that I would not be able to get free. The spirit of death had taken hold of me and I did not know how to free myself from its grip.

I had not previously considered suicide during the years of turmoil and pain; as a matter of fact, I fought against it with everything in me. But one day a dreadful event in the life of one of my friends triggered such a deep level of pain that I did not have any fight left in me. That night, in the middle of the night while my family slept, I went to each of my children and softly stroked their hair, weeping quietly over them with tears of "goodbye." I wanted to be their mommy and see them grow up so much, but since I could not get free from the immense torment and pain, I decided they would be better off without me. I knew Jeff would find a beautiful woman one day to take my place.

My thoughts and beliefs were not accurate or rational, but they felt more real than any other decision I could imagine. After a silent goodbye to each of my four children, I walked to my bedroom and watched my husband sleeping, thinking about how he deserved so much better than the shell of the person that he had married. Then I went into the bathroom and swallowed a bottle of prescription medicine. It seemed like the least messy way to go.

I sat on a sofa in my living room and waited for the medication to take effect. Normally just one of those pills would quickly put me to sleep, but after a couple of hours I was still awake. I could not figure out why I hadn't passed out; I could not understand how I could even still be alive.

As the sun was beginning to rise, I panicked that after several hours I was still alert. Jeff got up early to go to work and I said nothing to him about what I had done. After he left the house and it was almost time for my young kids to wake up, I was suddenly overcome with an overwhelming urge to sleep. Just then my phone rang. I let my answering machine pick up the call and heard the voice of my best friend saying "Kathi, are you around?" She never called me early in the morning, so I picked up the phone out of concern that something might have happened to her. As soon as she heard my voice, she asked what the matter was — she thought something sounded "off" in my voice. I didn't tell her what I had done but she knew something wasn't right. She hung up and called our mutual friend Aurora, who lived nearby, and asked her to go to my house and check on me. By the time Aurora arrived, I could no longer stay awake. She arranged for care for my kids and rushed me to the hospital. God had kept me awake until help could come to save my life.

I was in the hospital for several hours while doctors and nurses pumped my stomach and performed other procedures to stabilize me. Aurora called Jeff to tell him what happened, and he left work and raced to my side. My therapist arrived also, along with a couple of other close friends. Together they assured the medical staff that I would be closely supervised, and would not be alone at any time, so that I would not be a danger to myself or others. They released me with a stern warning to the others to continually monitor me.

In the days that followed, I was ashamed and mortified by what I had done. Coming home from the hospital after a failed suicide attempt was like getting plunged into the deepest shame one can ever imagine. Not only did I have no control over my emotions or my day-to-day life — I couldn't even succeed in killing myself! My friends looked at me differently and my husband was traumatized and had to step down from his pastoral position. And though I wouldn't have thought it possible, the longing to end my pain only increased. I felt wretched and degraded, filled with shame and guilt when I looked into the eyes of my precious children who did not deserve to have a mom in such despair. I carried on the next few days somehow, a ghost barely alive.

One afternoon about a week after my attempted suicide, several dear friends who had walked with me through the darkness for years called Jeff and asked if they could sit down with us to have an honest talk. He reluctantly agreed, so they gathered in our living room and we sat with them as they shared honestly and sorrowfully that they simply did not know what to do anymore. They did not see how they could do anything more to help me going forward from that point.

I sat stone-faced, impassive, not wanting to hear what they had to say, because I knew it was true, but I also felt utter panic. I had always been terrified that the day would come when everyone abandoned me. Now my fears were coming true.

As they continued to talk, I suddenly erupted with shame and desperation and fury. I jumped from my chair, grabbed my purse, and yanked my car keys from it. I turned to the group and swore at them, then stomped across the room and flung open my front door. Before I could cross the threshold, I suddenly heard a voice within me; ringing through my being so powerfully it was almost audible. It was the Lord speaking tenderly but firmly.

"Daughter, if you go out this door, you will die. Today you have a choice between life and death; so choose life."

I wavered for a moment but knew beyond a shadow of doubt that I had to choose life. To tear myself free from the grip of the spirit of death that was seemingly consuming me felt as though I would be ripped into pieces. With an act of sheer will (borne, I know now, by the power of the Holy Spirit) I grabbed the door jamb and forced myself back into the room and closed the door.

At first, I stood behind a chair near the front door, listening to Jeff and the others plead with me to understand that they all loved me and just did not want to see me in such bondage. I didn't say anything, and I was leaving my option to leave again open in case I changed my mind.

Eventually, I walked slowly across the room and sat back down, determined to stay and face whatever lay ahead of me, regardless of what it would cost me.

That was the point I allowed God to lift me from a black grave and allure me into the wilderness, where he could meet with me and would restore me.

My wilderness time was not easy, nor did it pass quickly. For nine months I spent hours each night just waiting before God until I would hear one word or feel one touch from him. It was as if I had to learn to live and to feel his presence again.

Some nights it would only take an hour or so; other nights I would sit waiting five or six hours before receiving what I needed to make it through another day.

I didn't realize it at the time, but this process was teaching me to overcome the destruction in my life as the Holy Spirit gently, patiently removed the grave clothes of death and shame layer by layer, replacing them with garments of beauty and life. I gradually found myself being strengthened and becoming healthy physically, emotionally, and spiritually over the nine-month period. It was if I was being recreated in the womb of his love. Every day the light was getting brighter, truth was getting clearer, and the door of hope was opening wider to me.

Grants Pass: the Thirty Days

Then in November, I was invited to a large conference in Grants Pass, Oregon. I honestly did not want to go but a group of ladies from my church insisted and even paid all my expenses. Jeff also encouraged me to go, so I couldn't say no. I made the necessary arrangements and a group of us made the six-hour drive, arriving just in time for the first evening session.

The conference was being held in a massive outdoor tent. As we walked in and found seats in the back of the crowded tent, I knelt to put my purse under my seat just as the worship leader strummed the first chord on his guitar. As if a bomb had exploded, I was knocked sprawling on the ground by the power of the Holy Spirit. I was shocked and disoriented, even as I was immediately overcome with his manifest presence. I began to shake uncontrollably and I could not get up. As worship continued, I felt like angels had surrounded me and were doing a divine work deep inside me. The worship set ended and the preaching began, and still I lay on the ground shaking. It continued through the entire service and did not lessen even as the night came to a close. My sweet friends recognized the work of the Spirit happening in me, so they graciously carried me to the car and then to my hotel room. That night the shaking continued as I felt the Lord's presence increasing more and more. By the next morning I felt as though I could feel his presence in the very cells of my body. I had not eaten since the previous afternoon, but I wasn't hungry or tired. I felt completely refreshed.

Once again, my friends had to carry me, and they helped me into the tent where they laid me on the ground for another full day of meetings. What was happening to me did not stop or lessen at all that day, and it continued the second night even as I slept. By the third day of the conference, my friends felt it was important to get some food into me since my body was in constant movement. They decided to take me to a restaurant next to the parking lot of the hotel where they could find a corner table, so my shaking would not be too much of a distraction. As they were escorting me to the back of the dining area, I heard a man's voice calling to us from one of the nearby tables. We turned to see the entire group of well-known prophetic ministers who were speaking at the conference sitting together. They beckoned to us to come over and smiled to see me sandwiched between two friends as they gripped my arms to keep me upright. One of the men asked what was happening. I told him that whatever it was, it started with the first strum of the guitar the first night and had not stopped for even a moment. Suddenly the whole group began to prophesy over me, saying God was breaking things off and putting things in and that it would continue for thirty days before the work was completed. Then one of them asked me to go around the table and lay hands on every man and woman sitting there because they all needed what was happening to me.

 Turned out, their prophecy was completely accurate, because the shaking and the overwhelming presence of God did not leave me for the next thirty days. I shook while I slept, throughout the day when I was awake and took care of the household, when I went to the store or ran errands, and in the evening as I prepared dinner. Some days it was difficult to function, but there was always grace to care for my children and to do what needed to be done through the busy holiday season. I was experiencing the manifest presence of God twenty-four hours a day for thirty days straight. By the time it ended I was having open-eyed visions and dreams every night, and the overwhelming joy of the Lord had raised me back to life. <u>I have never been the same.</u>

Unfortunately, there were individuals for whom my thirty-day experience was an opportunity for offense. We had some people at our church leave; others suggested that I could *make it stop*; and others said they just could not understand it and it didn't "seem like God." Honestly, I did not understand it either, and I did not desire this kind of attention, but I surely didn't want the amazing work being done inside of me to stop just to appease people. Most of the people in our church were overjoyed, and often what was happening to me would spill over onto them. Though we lost people, what we gained was an outpouring of his Spirit bringing us greater joy and life. Even our young children were being healed by it. They would laugh and worship and dance in his presence like never before.

I don't share this story to draw attention to myself or impress people with the extended encounter I had with God; but rather to illustrate how the progression took place. Once I was freed from the spirit of death, I entered a wild and unfamiliar place where the Lord spoke Hosea 2 over me. He allured me into the wilderness to restore me. During that time, I had to cooperate with him, but I know that most of the time he carried me because I was too weak to walk forward. He performed his miracles by saving me from my suicide attempt and delivering me from the spirit of death.

The nine months of staying awake every night was a process of simple trust. I would take a faltering step closer to him in the darkness and listen for one word or wait for even a momentary touch. That was my part in my wilderness journey. Although I didn't know it, the months of waiting were ushering me, step by step, closer to the door of hope that was about to be opened for me.

The wilderness is where we are purified, delivered, and restored so we can experience an outpouring of love. It requires waiting and patient trust in Jesus's divine work in our lives. Though it will look different for each person, and with each different wilderness season, it will always require partnership with the wonderful Holy Spirit. He will reveal simple things for you to do. Be sure to respond to his invitation because it will set you up for the coming outpouring of his love. It may not be as dramatic as my experience (or it might be even more astonishing!) but you can be sure it will be lovingly designed for you. Mine was crafted to bring me out of three years in the grip of the spirit of death.

When the thirty days were finished, so was my time in that wilderness. As I continued on, the Spirit spoke to me from Song of Solomon chapter 8:

Who is this coming up from the wilderness
leaning on her beloved?
Under the apple tree I roused you;
there your mother conceived you,
there she who was in labor gave you birth.
Place me like a seal over your heart,
like a seal on your arm;
for love is as strong as death,
its jealousy unyielding as the grave.
It burns like blazing fire,
like a mighty flame.
Many waters cannot quench love;
rivers cannot sweep it away.
If one were to give
all the wealth of one's house for love,
it would be utterly scorned.
Song of Solomon 8:5-7

This is the goal of all our journeying through the wilderness: to come out fully leaning upon our Beloved. He is our heart's true home.

The Door of Hope

God has set before us the choice of life or death. Though there are times that it does not feel like it is our choice, we are always offered a door of life to walk through. Close every door that leads to death and the sting of death. When the stone was rolled away from Jesus's grave, the Lord rolled away death and opened the way to resurrection life. This door open to you today: the door to life, the door to hope — the door that leads you home. Choose life!

CHAPTER SIX

the Door of Hope

Return to your fortress, you prisoners of hope; even now I announce that I will restore twice as much to you.
Zechariah 9:12

THROUGH THE YEARS I HAVE discovered a deeper meaning of the verse in Zechariah 9:12 that addresses the "prisoners of hope."

Return to your fortress — or in other words, *your place of safety*. For most of us, home is our place of safety, our fortress, our refuge. Yet, as Jesus told us, any home not built on the foundation of the rock of his words will fall when the storms of life come (Matthew 7:24-27). Therefore, it is important to build all our hopes upon the foundation provided by Jesus. We are bound to the eternal hope of the *yet to come* while living in the here and now. We are captives of hope living in a crumbling world, and yet we cannot separate ourselves from the eternal hope that is found in the kingdom yet to come, whose maker is Jesus. We are not merely prisoners of hope but prisoners who continuously *have* hope. This hope is eternal therefore it even spans beyond death.

Zechariah 9:12 goes on to say that God will restore double for all our trouble. Although he is addressing Israel in this verse, there remains a personal promise for all his sons and daughters. We know that in this world we will have tribulations and trials, greetings and partings, beginnings and endings; but we are to be of good cheer because Christ has overcome the world on our behalf and makes all things new. One day the greetings, beginnings, and good cheer will never end as we walk through our final door of hope into our eternal home.

I have come to realize as I have journeyed through life as a prisoner of hope that doors of hope are always opened before me when I go through troubles. Each door looks different than the one before, but each one leads to new and unexplored parts of experiences within the heart of God. Passing through the door of hope has always led me into double blessings for the troubles that came before. Often, the blessings become the fulfillment of unspoken hopes that only the Father would have known. They have been as doors of hope for me. I stumbled upon one door that day as a broken fourteen-year-old who first heard the sound of worship. I walked through another door in the moment of my broken engagement that led me to salvation and all things new. And I was carried over the threshold of another door the day that I walked into that conference tent after three years of pain; Jesus lifted me in his arms and walked with me into a life-changing encounter. Just as the wilderness is often unexpected, so are the beautiful doors of hope that God opens amid the Valley of Achor (Hosea 2:15; Joshua 7:24-26). Each time I was allured, enticed into the Valley of Trouble; yet there a door stood open for me that would lead me to the future and hope that he had planned for me.

Sharon shall become a pasture for flocks,
and the Valley of Achor a place for herds to lie down,

for my people who have sought me.
Isaiah 65:10, ESV

Sometimes the door of hope appears before you when you were not looking for it. The Spirit of God knows the deepest desires of our hearts even when we are not consciously aware of the longing of our souls. God was loving me and pursuing me before I even knew to look for him. He saw the deep longing of my heart and he knew I was searching for him even before I knew he was someone who could be found. **What mercy!**

Luke's Story

I watched God do the same thing for our son-in-law — the God of mercy pursued Luke even as he ran from him. I first met our future son-in-law when he was a broken and very confused teenager. My oldest son had met him while hanging out with some friends and discovered that he played guitar, so he invited him to our house to play with his band. Corey could see that he was a lost soul and probably needed some positive friendships. The day he came to our home the first time he was dressed in all black, wore black nail polish and eye liner, and had a shroud of darkness around him. Most of the kids that hung out at our home were Christian kids from church youth groups, so this was new for me to experience up close. This young man just wanted to play music and have a place to escape his home life, yet it seemed as if there was a silent cry in him that screamed, *"Help me. Rescue me. Love me!"*

At that time, our youngest daughter was a young teen, and I could see this young man acting flirtatious with her. For this reason, I was extremely hesitant about allowing him to be too close to our family. He was a very nice-looking teenager, with a guitar in hand and a charismatic personality. I could see her eyes light up when he walked into the room as she looked right past the dark shroud and outward warning signs. She had always been someone who would see the "garden" despite the "weeds" in hurting people and she could only see the garden that needed to be tended in him. This is how she was wired — to see the potential and good within each person. But at fourteen years old, Luke's life was not a garden I wanted to see her tending to.

But he was persistent in his pursuit of having relationship with our family. I was convinced that it was motivated by wanting a relationship with our daughter, so Jeff and I firmly resisted his attempts to build relationship out of protection for her heart and purity. Yet, the Lord was pursuing him with a love that could not be resisted. Jeff and I finally agreed to have him over so that we could share our faith and why we would not allow a relationship with our daughter. During that meeting, I was having constant encounters with God's love for him, seeing God's plans for him and his pursuit of him. Though this young man had no desire for God — quite the opposite, in fact — God was not deterred. While the young man spoke with us that evening, I suddenly heard a voice in my spirit that said, *"Kathi, will you raise your son-in-law?"*

I rebuked the voice and said, *"No, this is not who my daughter will marry! Her husband will be a man after God's heart and that will protect her pure heart."*

Then I was shown vision of him in the future playing his guitar in worship and speaking to teens about the redemptive love of God. I finally, and reluctantly, said "Yes" to God's request. (I kept the part about *raising my son-in-law* between the Lord and me; I wasn't about to spring that on Jeff! Also,

I hoped I was wrong and really hadn't heard correctly.)

I discovered that this young man had been raised in a pastor's home but what was spoken on Sunday mornings was not lived out the rest of the week. Their home life was turbulent, painful, and filled with things that contradicted the nice words spoken in church services. Hypocrisy was all he knew, and that had become his belief about Christians. Eventually, one day while his dad was at work, his mom took him and his sister and left their home, leaving behind their beloved dogs and everything Luke had known. This became a pattern in their lives in the years that followed. Luke had no contact with his dad, and his mom moved from city to city, always leaving behind everything they owned. This re-occurring loss of everything precious to him marked his soul with disconnection and rage. He claimed to *hate* his mother and *hate* God. He was utterly broken and lost, but deep inside he longed for a family and a home. On more than one occasion I watched him weep uncontrollably when the brokenness would overwhelm him.

In the months that followed, Luke became a part of our family. He rarely went back to the empty apartment where his mom lived, and he opted to stay in our son's room more often than not. He just wanted a home and a family. Because he was failing high school, I decided to home school him and search for a way to get beyond the darkness with the help of the Holy Spirit. Slowly but surely, his heart began to soften and respond to the love of his heavenly Father. God walked into the dark wilderness of his life and presented a door of hope to him — even when he was not looking for it. Over time his heart began to heal, and he humbled himself before Jesus. This young man who claimed to hate God and hate life responded to the love of the Father that was revealed to him day by day until he decided to through that door of hope. Our daughter and he married in October 2011, and he has traveled the nation playing his guitar in worship bands. This year marks their ten-year anniversary, and I can honestly say our daughter received a husband after God's heart, who longs to protect the purity of her heart as well. It has not been a perfect journey on a smooth road, but it has been a pilgrimage to the heart of God, filled with redemption and promise.

Always remember that you are always being fervently pursued by a love that never gives up on you. You took the breath of God away from first moment he saw you. When you asked him into your life as your savior, it was like a young man's first glance at the girl that would steal his heart. From the moment that your heart is joined to his, it is also joined to his plans for you — to give you a future and to open the door of hope before you. He is continually orchestrating the details of your steps to prosper your body, soul, and spirit. Some of the paths he orchestrates lead us into what we perceive as valleys of trouble and yet it is there that you are once again prepared to cross over the threshold of a new door of hope. Within that door of hope he has set a table for you that is plated with promises and hopes fulfilled.

Everything that he does is for the good of his sons and daughters — or for those who will one day become adopted sons and daughters. As prisoners of hope, we are bound within the covenant of his love, which is eternal. And his covenant of love contains a double portion of every promise spoken of within his Word; whether realized in this world or in the kingdom yet to come. Whenever you travel a path through a dry and thirsty wilderness, you can be sure Jesus will always stand as the door of hope to usher you into greater things.

The Door of Hope

Jesus is forever pursuing you! There has never been a day that his love has not been chasing you down. He longs for you to experience all that he has for you and all that he has prepared for you. You are never separated from hope — the cross bound you to a hope that follows you all the days of your life.

CHAPTER SEVEN

Coming Out of Egypt

Now the rabble that was among them had a strong craving. And the people of Israel also wept again and said, "Oh that we had meat to eat! We remember the fish we ate in Egypt that cost nothing, the cucumbers, the melons, the leeks, the onions, and the garlic. But now our strength is dried up, and there is nothing at all but this manna to look at."
Numbers 11:4-6, ESV

In 1980, Keith Green wrote a song titled "So You Wanna Go Back to Egypt?" that poked good-natured, but pointed, fun at the children of Israel and their complaints. The lyrics are comical, as the unnamed narrator laments about their wilderness wanderings: questioning why they left Egypt only to encounter hot sand, being "forced" to eat only manna day after day, and living through the dreadful experience of the golden cow.

The correlations with our culture and attitudes are readily apparent. How quickly we forget our captivity and begin to romanticize where we came from. I do not know why people feel the grass is always greener elsewhere, but we surely do. We forget that our "Egypt" was where we were enslaved to harsh and cruel taskmasters who used us only for what benefitted them.

Today we are observing humanity in another desert place where grumbling and complaining seems to be the conversation of the day. The complaints of today day are over masks, restrictions regarding indoor dining, political parties, differences of opinions; prophetic voices have spoken to the church and said that the Promised Land is ahead — but at the moment we only see hot and barren desert. (Have we considered that perhaps we only have a short, temporary desert walk to the Promised Land?) We long for where we were in former years saying, "Can't we have 2017, 2018, or even 2019 back? Or better yet, let us go back to the 80's or 90's when times seemed simpler." Yet, with every step and every day forward we are further away from our former captivity. We are pressing onward towards the Promised Land that flows with milk and honey — the New Jerusalem.

Will we harden our hearts like the Israelites that were not permitted to enter the land of promise? Will we stay behind and build a golden calf while modern-day Moseses ascend the mountain to meet with God? God forbid that we do not learn the lessons from biblical history! What if this desert is the wilderness that God has called us into so that he can restore us? What if it is here that he will remove the names of Baals (masters) from us so that we will once again call him "Husband." What if this is the place where we will see peace, safety, righteousness, justice, and compassion from forth? We must turn our eyes upon Jesus and not look back at Egypt.

Your "Egypt" does not necessarily represent the time before your salvation. It can represent any place that holds you back from the fullness of God's promises over your life. As we have discussed in previous chapters, captivity can come in subtle ways that are not connected with deliberate or even conscious choices. Some people have strongholds of perfection that leads to a captivity of guilt and feelings of failure; others deal with strongholds of pride that lead them to unwanted faltering and judgmental attitudes; and still others live with strongholds of rejection that lead to a captivity of shame and self-hatred. Sometimes these strongholds are like an onion that needs to be peeled layer by layer. I have found that the removal of these layers happens most often in the wilderness as we become still and yield to the work of the Holy Spirit. We were not created for captivity but for freedom and Jesus will settle for nothing less within his bride.

It is for freedom that Christ has set us free. Stand
firm, then, and do not let yourselves be burdened again
by a yoke of slavery.
Galatians 5:1

As *prisoners of hope* we are not held captive to a harsh taskmaster, but we are yoked to freedom through Christ Jesus. He already paid our penalty and defeated every master — even death. Jesus came to take the heavy yoke from tired and weary sojourners traveling through this world and replace it with his light and easy yoke.

"Come to me, all you who are weary and burdened,
and I will give you rest. Take my yoke upon you and
learn from me, for I am gentle and humble in heart,
and you will find rest for your souls. For my yoke is
easy and my burden is light."
Matthew 11:29-30

"Will you Leave the Door Open?"

In chapter five, I wrote about my "dark night of the soul" that included a suicide attempt. For many years leading up to that experience, I was held captive by the eating disorder I mentioned in my introduction.

Bulimia was a heavy yoke and a harsh taskmaster over my life. I had not allowed Jesus to take the burden of shame from me; therefore I allowed this "master" to demand that I wear a yoke that was too much for me to bear. Even after becoming a wife, entering ministry, and becoming a mom it ruled my life day after day. It was a secret that no one knew about — not even Jeff. It had its roots in my wrong responses to pain and fear in my childhood.

When I was a young girl, my dad was extremely angry because of the disintegration of our family life and the dreadful animosity between he and my mom. When he became enraged, he would sometimes take his fury out on me. I would hear his recliner suddenly slam closed followed by the sound of his belt being pulled from his pants, which signaled to me that it was time to run. I became good at outrunning him. I knew that if I could get to the bathroom faster than he could get to me, I could lock the door and be safe until his nightly routine of burgundy and beer lulled him to sleep, or at least into enough of a stupor that he was no longer stirred up. Alcohol calmed him, but sobriety left him angry and bitter.

I spend countless hours sitting on the floor of our bathroom while growing up. It became a place of temporary safety, but it also became a place where the father of lies sat on his throne and whispered lies of shame to me.

I believed them all. Over the years I became convinced that my only hope of being loved was through having a body that was attractive because I did not believe that there was any good thing within me. If my own father did not love me, then how could anyone? The truth is that my dad did love me — but he had not been shown much affection by his parents and he was also consumed with self-hatred and shame that had turned to rage. The guilt he felt about how he acted only pushed him farther away from me.

The years of sitting and listening to lies had destroyed my soul. One day I was so scared and ashamed that I became nauseous and I threw up. Afterwards I felt immediate relief from the fear and shame. It was as if I had just vomited out all the negative emotions that were tormenting my soul. The next time these feelings overwhelmed me I purged them as before; and again the relief was immediate and I felt in control.

Eventually the only way to rid myself of the consuming shame was through throwing up. This became my way of coping with chaos, and it was the way I could feel a short time of relief.

Purging shame became a daily ritual that I brought into my new life in Christ, into my marriage, and into motherhood. I believed that when I went into the bathroom it was the place that even my heavenly Father could not enter. I was able to separate this act so thoroughly from my life that I did not even consider it sin or a "real" problem. No one was allowed in there but me and the voice of the father of lies, which I thought was my voice.

During my second pregnancy the struggle with my secret coping skill intensified. I had been able to resist during my first pregnancy but did not seem to be able to stop during this pregnancy. We were so excited to have another little one join our family and I felt that I needed to be able to cope with, and keep, my emotions in control. I tried hard to resist the urge to give into bulimia but often I found the addiction stronger than me.

In the fifth month of my pregnancy, I woke up one morning and something didn't seem right. I had felt our baby kicking the night before, but this morning I felt odd, and I realized the baby hadn't moved all morning. I went into the bathroom discovered that I was bleeding. I was instantly terrified. Jeff called the doctor and she said to wait and see if it stopped, but over the next couple hours the bleeding got increasingly worse. We took our two children to a friends house and rushed to our doctor, and we waited in the exam room for what felt like forever. We were so anxious and scared. Finally, the doctor came in to examine me and found that there was no heartbeat. It was like we were suddenly in our worst nightmare. We sat dumbly in disbelief, absolutely devastated.

I was transferred to a nearby hospital where they performed a procedure to take our precious little girl out of my body. Both Jeff and I were overwhelmed with grief and all the while I wondered if my inability to completely stop purging had contributed to our daughter's death. I will never know for sure if her death was my fault, but this tragic and heartbreaking miscarriage caused me, for the first time, to decide to fight against this deadly way of controlling my emotions.

Unfortunately, the shame and pain I was now carrying was even greater, even as I consciously fought against my form of coping. I still had never told anyone about it. So I would have seasons of successfully resisting, standing firm for a time and not resorting to purging; then I would enter another season of giving in. All the while, I struggled in secret, until I eventually ended up in a treatment center.

I wrote how after my suicide attempt and my deliverance from the spirit of death, I sought the Lord night after night for a touch that would allow me to keep living. Even though I gradually found myself being restored to life through many sleepless hours, I still had not been set free from bulimia.

It was near the end of my nine-month period of crying out that the story I opened this book with happened.

That particular morning Jeff was at work and my kids were at a friend's house playing. I felt the familiar shame build up once again, but I fought the temptation to purge the pain until I could no longer take it.

But the mercy I was about to experience wiped away the torments of the past. The Lord began with that simple request:

"Daughter, will you leave the door open?"

His wisdom is infinite and his lovingkindness is unfathomable. Romans 2:4 tells us that God is "rich" in kindness and forbearance and patience, and that his kindness is meant to lead us to repentance. His delivered me through his mercy when he knelt with me and said, *"Kathi, from now on, I will always be here with you."*

It was about a month later I had the experience in Grants Pass that was to completely change the trajectory of my life.

As I look at the body of Christ, it is obvious that letting go of the heavy yokes that weary us is not an easy thing. The devil wants to keep God's people enslaved under burdens, anxiety, strife, and exhaustion. He always seeks to *wear down the saints of God* (Daniel 7:25) through accusations that cause us to despair of freedom and turn back into captivity. He will whisper that God does not notice us or care; that he is unfaithful, deaf, silent, or angry. He says we are unloved, condemned, and full of shame. He will twist the troubling circumstances in our lives and then point to God as the one who brought them upon his people.

We are all subject to this wearing down process, yet there is a way to resist this enemy of God and his saints.

That way is to take God at his Word.

There are many times throughout my life that I have not understood why things happened to me or someone I loved that brought deep pain. Was it the enemy? Did God permit it? And why? I have had to settle in my heart that he is forever faithful, and even if I do not understand or have the answers to my questions, I choose to believe that he is who he says that he is. *"He is forever faithful"* is my answer to the questions that have no answers.

Reject every accusation that is brought against God. If the words you are hearing do not align with who the Scriptures say he is, then you need to reject those words. When you begin to entertain them as possibly true, allowing your heart to meditate on the accusations, an agreement is created, and the enemy has a doorway to destroy your hope. When you resist the enemy and his accusations, they have no hold on you, and you remain free. God had offered me freedom from the shame and pain of my past when I came to know him, and yet I believed lies about myself, and him, so I took constant trips back to Egypt and captivity for so many years.

Egypt can be described as any yoke of slavery that rests upon our life. The Spirit of God is the greatest advocate for our freedom. He is relentless about seeing us free to live as prisoners of hope in the secure grip of his unconditional love. We can ask him to remove the name of every "master" who has been ruling places in our lives. The Lord is our Moses, our Deliverer, the One who says to the masters who rule over us with heavy burdens, *"Let My people go!"*

You were not made to live in Egypt. You were created for

Eden. The door of hope in the wilderness is open and you will find your Father there waiting for you. The wilderness seasons will often serve to usher you to the door that takes you into the Eden he has created you for — your true home.

A Personal Word for You

As I finished writing this chapter, I heard a personal word for those of you reading this who are weary:

Some of you are so very weary right now. Jesus wants you to know how deep his compassion is toward you. He is with you right where you are, with no expectations, except for you to allow him to love you and give you rest.

Some of you are so very burdened right now. The weight of what you are carrying is crushing you, but you feel that if your strength fails, everything will fall to the ground and crumble. Jesus wants you to know how deep his compassion is for you. He is with you right where you are to remove the yoke and burden that you are carrying. He will trade it for his yoke, which is merely to trust him for all you need and all that you are carrying. Remember the words from Matthew 11:28-30,

> "Come to Me, all of you who are weary and burdened, and I will give you rest. All of you, take up My yoke and learn from Me, because I am gentle and humble in heart, and you will find rest for yourselves. For My yoke is easy and My burden is light."

The Father is so gentle with you. His Son is the perfect example of having the fullness of being "humble in heart" toward you. He is inviting you to come into his arms and receive the rest that you so desperately need.

He has healing for your heart, provision for all that you need, and restoration for every trauma and circumstance that has hurt you and caused you to feel that you must carry this heavy burden. He loves you so very much— he knows you intimately, every part of you, and yes, he still loves you; you take his breath away. He is pouring out the abundance of his love over you even now. Let go of the control, the yoke that has wearied you, and let your pain fall into his lap. He wants to carry you and refresh you in his love.

Receive his love. He is gentle and humble in heart.

the Door of Hope

Jesus has so much compassion for all that you have gone through in your life. Often, we create closed doors or walls that are built upon shame and a misunderstanding of who he is and how he loves us. You can now open the door and tear down the walls of shame that you have constructed to keep him from seeing the depravity within you. He longs to come in so that he can pour out his compassion upon you. It is a compassion that heals you. You can touch the hem of his garment even now, as he frees you from your prison of shame and welcomes you into the freedom of your Father's home.

CHAPTER EIGHT

Responding in Stillness

There she will respond as in the days of her youth,
as in the day she came up out of Egypt.
Hosea 2:15

I STARTED DATING JEFF IN 1982. Young love is fresh
and full of dreams; you are excited to be around the other
person — attentive to every little invitation, quick to respond to your beloved's voice. I remember a friend coming
to me to complain that Jeff and I spent all our time with
each other and seemed to avoid time with other friends. I
did not apologize. We loved our friends, but we were in the
enchantment of new love and responding to each other was
our greatest joy. Now, after almost four decades of sharing
life together, we must remind ourselves to set time aside
to be alone together, to be still and respond to one another with sensitivity and honor. Our love is so much deeper
now; it is an abiding love, but it is no longer new, and sometimes we can slip into a settled comfort that can cause us to
take the other person for granted.

It is possible for this to happen in our relationship with
Jesus. We become so caught up in what he has revealed to
us and the work of his kingdom that we forget to culti-
vate wonder. We forget to come to him with love and trust
that responds with awe-filled gratitude at the delight of his
presence. *Therefore, he allures us into the wilderness — to re-*

ignite our desire to respond to him with excitement and enthusiasm, without hesitation.

My obedience to his voice can never replace the intimate response that says "yes" out of sheer longing.

> Now as they went on their way, Jesus entered a village.
> And a woman named Martha welcomed him into her
> house. And she had a sister called Mary, who sat at
> the Lord's feet and listened to his teaching. But Mar-
> tha was distracted with much serving. And she went
> up to him and said, "Lord, do you not care that my
> sister has left me to serve alone? Tell her then to help
> me." But the Lord answered her, "Martha, Martha,
> you are anxious and troubled about many things, but
> one thing is necessary. Mary has chosen the good por-
> tion, which will not be taken away from her."
> Luke 10:38-42

It can be so difficult to be quiet and listen for Jesus's voice in our incredibly busy and stressful culture. I have discovered that the wilderness is a place that nurtures and reignites stillness and grateful response. In the wilderness I find myself letting go of constant activities, even spiritual activities, and getting still so that I can listen and grow to know him more. It is by saying "Peace, be still!" to my normally restless heart that I find once again that *he alone is God.* The stilling of my soul usually involves a wrestle with my flesh to cease striving from my thoughts, my ideas, and my *wisdom.* It also involves a wrestle against the subtle but nevertheless pervasive impression that somehow God needs me. The truth is that he desires me, but he is perfectly able to function without me. It is his desire to be with me and to invite me into all that he does, but he can do it all without me. What a joy to know that he desires us rather than needs us.

The Power of Simplicity

When the Holy Spirit breathes his thoughts and dreams into my heart and mind, it is so much better and wiser than any of my ponderings. But if I start taking responsibility to "make things happen" and abandon the posture of abiding trust, I do not feel a release or greater confidence after praying — *I merely feel as though I have not done enough.* In his kindness, God pulls me out of the chaos of my own whirlwind of thoughts and emotions, and the demands of self-dependence, and once again calls me into stillness.

In March of 2020, as the pandemic hit our nation with panic and national shutdowns, I still in his presence I was taken into a vision that set the course for my year.

In the vision I saw Jesus walking up to a door set into a human heart. He began to gently knock on the door, and I saw the woman — the heart's owner — get up quickly to answer his knock. She opened the door and invited the Lord to come in, but he surveyed the area and found there was no room. Her heart was packed with "spiritual paraphernalia." There were books, teachings, notes, papers, artwork, workbooks, training manuals, and calendars. Her heart was filled with so much information about him that there was no room for him. He asked her if he could clear the room so he could come in. She responded immediately, "Yes Lord." He quickly removed all her possessions until there was nothing left. With the area cleared, he brought in a wooden table and two chairs. Then he placed a loaf of bread and a cup of wine on the table, and he sat down and invited her to join him. As she sat down, he looked at her with such tenderness and love, and said, "This is all you need."

This vision was not only personal, but it was a picture of what God was about to do in his bride. In 2020 I experienced a year of communion with my King. It was intimate, beautiful, and restoring. The simple truth of his blood and body, and his presence with me, truly became all that I needed. My response was merely, *"Yes Lord."* I asked him to come and take all of me, I did not want to hold anything back or depend on anything I had learned beyond Christ and him crucified.

> For I resolved to know nothing while I was with you
> except Jesus Christ and him crucified.
> 1 Corinthians 2:2

I am not against books or teaching (after all, you are reading my book!) but nothing can replace the simple truth of the gospel. I believe we sometimes become so impressed with our own knowledge that we forget the pure message that our salvation was obtained *for us;* Jesus needed no help from us to accomplish "so great a salvation" (Hebrews 2:3).

There are times in my life I have become aware I was trying to use wise and persuasive words rather than ask for a demonstration of the Spirit's power through the message of the cross of Christ. His power inhabits our words when we proclaim the truth of his testimony and his work in our lives. When I don't depend on my wisdom or ability to persuade, he comes with a demonstration of power. My life and other's lives are changed by his authority, not by my wisdom.

Therefore, we give him all — all our wisdom, our knowledge, our sin, our failures, our longings, our dreams, our *authority.* We want Christ and him crucified to be the doorway to home.

Time in the wilderness sheds us of self-inflicted burdens and restores us to dependent trust, leaning on our Beloved.

Trust in the LORD with all your heart and lean not

on your own understanding; in all your ways submit
to him, and he will make your paths straight.
Proverbs 3:5-6

The moment that we begin to lean on our own understanding our paths will be marked by blind corners and precarious twists and turns. Why? Because our ways are not his ways, and without his wisdom we lack clear sight. So what appears to us to be a smooth path ends up a dangerous slippery slope. The straight road we think we are following turns out to be a rocky path that leads to confusion. As we lean on him, he takes us by the hand and leads us on a straight path. We see his wisdom through eyes of trust and we walk without stumbling with a posture of complete dependency.

We can often be guilty of this mistake in the prophetic community. We will be given a powerful prophetic experience, or hear a significant prophetic word, and then try to figure out the best way to see that word accomplished. In my experience, I have almost never been right about how these prophetic promises or words will be fulfilled by God. I have learned to get my heart and mind still until I can rest in his wisdom so that I do not venture off on a winding path that only leads me to a wilderness that he did not allure me into. Of course, if that happens, he is with me there as well, but such detours are full of hidden snares and our loving Father deeply desires to keep us free from harm. Surrender is much better than striving.

I have had to learn many different ways of getting still through the years. (I write about a recent time in the next chapter.) One of the first times God called me to intentional stillness was when he was setting me free from worry and anxiety. I had struggled with those issues for years and God no longer wanted me to live in the snare of anxious thoughts, fear, and unbelief. He wanted me to live in the joy that his perfect love provides for all his sons and daughter. At the time God began touching this area, our family was living out of the country and being provided for through mission support. Our committed monthly support was about a quarter of what we needed to meet expenses. I found myself losing sleep, feeling continually grumpy, and experiencing anxiety and panic almost daily. It was so bad that I often fantasized returning home and living a "normal" life, turning away from what God had asked us to do.

His dealing with my anxious heart began one day when I clearly sensed the Holy Spirit's quiet, insistent prompting: *"Kathi, I want you to be still."*

My mind was spinning with a multitude of concerns and questions, and it didn't seem possible to quiet my anxiety enough to be "still"! So I asked the Lord, "What does that look like?"

He answered my question with a question, *"What would you feel like if you had more than enough finances for everything that you need?"*

That one was easy. "My stomach wouldn't be twisted in knots; my heart would stop pounding, and I could think of something other than trying to figure out how we are going to make ends meet."

If I had enough money, I could stop "helping" God and reminding him of our needs — I would just enjoy the day.

I could feel his kind and gentle correction as he said, *"Kathi, you have everything you need and more. Be still and trust me so you can enjoy each day."*

This seems simple, but my lifelong habit of worrying was hard to break. My Father was simply telling me to take every anxious thought and exchange it for the spiritual reality and ✷ promise of his unseen provision. With the help of the Holy Spirit, each day I was able to take those anxious thoughts captive and shift my posture from unbelief and fear to trust and peace. And for the first time, our family began to not only have enough, but often more than enough. I was stilling my mind and anxious heart and teaching myself to trust what he had spoken to me. What soon occurred was a deliverance from fear of abandonment. All through practicing ✷ stillness and trust.

A Call to Stillness

Have you ever tried to change the clothes on a baby who would not lie still? Most of us moms have gone through this process more times than we can count. It is like a wrestling match that draws out the whole process much longer than it needs to be. I remember many times, a baby "blow out," was followed by one of these wrestling matches. As my baby struggled (resisting my nurturing help) I wondered if he even cared that he was covered in filth and that his resistance was only making it worse. Did he not want to be clean? Did he not want to smell fresh again? Did he not want to feel the comfort of new garments?

Does this sound familiar? Are some of you going through a season that God is asking you to be still? Though this stillness may be an internal stillness of your soul rather than an external stillness from physical activity, it still seems to incite resistance in most people. We wrestle against the very hand that has come to help us, nurture us, and make us clean.

Maybe just like babies, we do not know that the garments of our soul have become soiled by the accuser. Maybe we do not like to be stripped of behavior patterns and beliefs we have become comfortable in. Perhaps we simply hate to be still and trust the hand that is changing us! It is possible that you have outgrown the garments you have been wearing and need new ones that fit who you have become. Many of God's children are in a time of being "changed." Do not fight the process but trust the hand that is washing you and putting new garments on you.

> *Silence is one of the deepest disciplines of the Spirit simply because it puts the stopper on all self-justification. One of the fruits of silence is the freedom to let God be our justifier.*[1]

When my kids were babies, I would often stop after removing their garments and before dressing them in new clothes, I would get lotions or oils and give them a massage. At first, they would often begin trying to flip over to get away but once my hands began to massage their little feet, legs, hands, and arms they would lay back in peace. When it was done, they were so relaxed that dressing them was easy.

God may be doing the same thing for you. He has not only removed your soiled garments and washed you, but he is restoring peace and relaxation — rest for your over-active soul. He is restoring trust so that you will receive all that is in his hands for you. He is cleansing, purifying, anointing, and healing you and changing your garments. The winter garments are about to be changed into garments suitable

---

1   Richard J. Foster, "Seeking the Kingdom Quotes," Goodreads, accessed July 28, 2021, https://www.goodreads.com/work/quotes/250461-seeking-the-kingdom-devotions-for-the-daily-journey-of-faith

for spring! Some of you are having grave clothes removed and are being adorned in resurrection outfits. A change of seasons is coming for you. Leaves will suddenly appear, blossoms will spring forth, and the grass will turn green once again. His Spirit is moving inside of you to bring new life! Though you do not see it now, be still because your fight and wrestle are only delaying the birthing of this new season. Take time to enjoy his tender touch, his washing; and then watch and see how he has chosen to adorn you. Even the angels have gathered around you to assist and watch the beauty that comes forth in you. Get still and receive from his tender hand.

"Be still and know that I am God..."
Psalm 46:10

the Door of Hope

Is the room of your heart cluttered? Do you long for Jesus to come and perform his cleaning? You can invite him by opening your door wide and inviting him to have his way. Stillness comes as we trust him, expressing our confident expectation of good from a Savior who purchased our life with love that we will never fully comprehend this side of heaven. Often, we hide areas of our lives behind unbelief, which creates restlessness and uneasiness. Open the door of trust that abandons all unbelief and rests in the warmth of his embrace. He comes to welcome you and draw you into his peace, where you are truly home and you know that he alone is God.

CHAPTER NINE

In the Waiting

Yes, as a people we are spoiled. We look for dinners
that take two minutes to cook in our microwave
instead of five, and we audibly sigh if the directions
on the box require us to stir at the halfway point. Aw,
I gotta stir? See what else is in the freezer.
Martha Bolton, *I Think,*
Therefore I have a Headache!

Stillness is hard for us. We want to be productive; many of us thrive on being busy. We think: *Yes, Mary sat at Jesus's feet and it was right, but Martha's conscientious service wasn't necessarily wrong!*

Of course we trust in God; but we still have responsibilities and deadlines. There is always so much to be done, and it seems not enough time to do it all. Plus, at heart most of us are impatient.

A few years ago my entire family traveled to visit our extended family in California. It promised to be a special time with family we had not seen in a long time. As we were preparing for the trip, I heard the Spirit of God whisper a request, *"Will you stay home and be with me?"*

I know the voice of my Beloved, so I had no doubt that this was a personal and intimate request. I struggled with it because I didn't know when, or if, there would be another gathering like this since some of our aunts and uncles were in their eighties.

The Lord's tender invitation lingered in my heart until I made the decision to yield to his request.

After my family left and I found myself in our home completely alone, I realized that it had been years since I had days alone with just my Savior. I went to my bedroom with my Bible and a pillow and lay down prostrate before him. And waited. He initiated the invitation, so I did not want to come with any agenda except to be with him. I waited while my heart and mind got still from all of life's activities — the daily "busy-ness" that clutters intimacy. The waiting seemed to take forever, but I knew that it was a necessary process to rid myself of my thoughts, my prayers, and my distractions. When my soul was finally still a flood of his love rushed in like a wave that immersed me. I immediately began weeping because it was so sweet and so strong. For hours I lay on the floor, saturated with nothing but his love and presence. I discovered that he, too, had no agenda except to be with me. It took the waiting to separate me from my cluttered soul that always seemed to have an agenda. My mind is always so full and busy that it takes great effort for all the "wheels" to stop turning. He was so patient with me as angels assisted him in dividing soul and spirit so that I could meet with him. When he came I had no words I could use to respond; only tears as I encountered his touch, his love, and his longing for me. The entire time that my family was gone was only about loving and being loved — his love for me and mine for him.

After those days something was opened in my spirit that allowed me to go to new depths in intercession. I could once again connect with the depths of his heart in a pure way that was free of the clutter of me. It became intercession that went beyond words, beyond understanding, yet it touched the very heart of God. He was in the waiting.

This is an exercise we all should probably do far more frequently, because life has a way of busying our mind and cluttering our thoughts. We are faithful to pray but often we do not *wait* on God. We will wait in coffee lines, amusement park lines and DMV (Department of Motor Vehicle) lines — but putting time aside to wait for the Spirit to clear our thoughts and sort through the clutter of our souls so we can meet with him does not seem to be high on our priority list. I know people who, once a year, put aside time to go alone to a remote place *just to meet with him.* Even then, we will often have agendas, such as finding out what he wants us to focus on that year. That is not a bad thing, but we often tend to make such times more like a business board meeting to discuss the year ahead.

What about just waiting to meet with him? We do that with our spouses. We even do that with close friends. What about our God?

Waiting seems to be exceedingly difficult for people; especially in the days that we are living in. We are trained to expect immediate results and to have our desires met without delay and without effort. We want "fast everything!" Fast food, fast cars, fast internet — you name it. Whatever it is, we want it *now.* We can meet with a friend without leaving our house and we can order a meal sent to our front door without seeing anyone. A heart emoji has replaced "I love you" and a quick text has replaced a phone call or hand-written letter. This has created a deficit in our character and in our ability to have patience and endurance. Waiting requires both.

> *Not only so, but we also glory in our sufferings, because we know that suffering produces perseverance; perseverance, character; and character, hope. And*

> *hope does not put us to shame, because God's love has*
> *been poured out into our hearts through the Holy*
> *Spirit, who has been given to us.*
> *Romans 5:3-5*

To walk through a wilderness is to spend extended times of waiting, and usually doing without.

Since it seems that we consider waiting to be suffering, then we need to allow the suffering of waiting in patience have its way in our lives. I cannot imagine what our younger generations must go through as they have been raised in a "have it now" environment. Our culture thrives on instant gratification. Some of us "older folks" have had a taste of that, but nothing like those who are thirty and under. Our kids haven't even had to learn to read a map because they have GPS at their fingertips. They have experienced the astonishing acceleration of modern technologies from birth.

I have watched many young people struggle to walk in perseverance and endurance and their exertion often wearies them to a point of hopelessness. Waiting is far more painful and difficult for them in our "lightning fast" society. There is no shortcut to the deep places in the heart of God. Reaching those secret places takes time; it takes waiting. How heartbreaking that we have robbed our children of this learned skill. They have been set up — programmed — to give up and become ashamed as hopelessness overcomes them. That is why the suicide rate in the younger generation, even among believers, is so high. The anxiety they experience when things do not come quickly overwhelms them, panic from the non-stop lifestyle of social media, and little face-to-face intimacy with God and other people has stolen peace and compassion from their life experiences.

Oh, that they would become aware of his alluring them into the wilderness to restore them to himself and to show them the door of hope. But the wilderness is not a place of instant gratification or answers; it is a posture of stillness and waiting. Transformation is not a momentary work; it takes time and patience. (If you are a young person reading this, do not feel shame or discouragement. Ask the Holy Spirit to restore to you the art of waiting and the compassion experienced in the quiet place with the Lord. He is waiting, he is patient, and his love for you endures forever.)

Look again at Romans 5:3-5 on the previous page. The verses reveal a clear and linear process that occurs in times of suffering. Although we do not boast of our sufferings, we glory in them because we are given an opportunity to gain great treasures in times of suffering. Suffering produces an ability to endure and not give up. This life skill is woven into our character in such a way that in extended times of perseverance through suffering, we do not lose hope.

We can see the devil's strategy in robbing people living today of these treasures that keep them in hope — the hope that does not disappoint. How tragic that we are watching young pastors and ministers take their lives because the pressures are so great, and they did not have the opportunity to know how to cope and grow from suffering. Their suffering led to despair rather than perseverance, character, and hope.

We cannot deny that we have not done a particularly good job of seeing how this fast moving, instant gratification world has left the younger generations in a wake of hopeless despair. The hysterical, hectic pace of our culture has taken its toll on all of us. We are sick with longing for the Lord's presence, and we desire to truly dwell there. Our hearts ache for face-to-face time with him, where we find peace once again. Psalm 84 is the cry of our hearts.

> *How lovely is your dwelling place,*
>   *Lord Almighty!*
> *My soul yearns, even faints,*
>   *for the courts of the Lord;*
> *my heart and my flesh cry out*
>   *for the living God.*
> ⭐ *Even the sparrow has found a home,*
>   *and the swallow a nest for herself,*
>   *where she may have her young—*
>   ⭐ *a place near your altar,*
> *Lord Almighty, my King and my God.*
> *Blessed are those who dwell in your house;*
>   *they are ever praising you.*
>
> ⭐ *Blessed are those whose strength is in you,*
>   *whose hearts are set on pilgrimage.*
> *As they pass through the Valley of Baka,*
>   *they make it a place of springs;*
>   *the autumn rains also cover it with pools.*
> ⭐ *They go from strength to strength,*
>   *till each appears before God in Zion.*
>
> *Hear my prayer, Lord God Almighty;*
>   *listen to me, God of Jacob.*
> *Look on our shield, O God;*
>   *look with favor on your anointed one.*
>
> *Better is one day in your courts*
>   *than a thousand elsewhere;*
> *I would rather be a doorkeeper in the house of my God*
>   *than dwell in the tents of the wicked.*
> *For the Lord God is a sun and shield;*

the Lord bestows favor and honor;
✦ *no good thing does he withhold*
from those whose walk is blameless.

Lord Almighty,
blessed is the one who trusts in you.

Our hearts longs for his courts. We long to take days where we do nothing but linger in his presence and behold him. Nothing is wasted in the waiting — waiting without expecting anything but to know him and to be known by him, just as we did when love was new.

It is time to rediscover the absolute beauty and peace that comes in the waiting. We must recognize those times that God is calling us to stop, wait, and find him once again in nothing but the purity of who he is, rather than what he does. The art of waiting will transform your life. It will free you from all that has enslaved you, controlled you, and pulled you away from intimacy.

But they who wait for the Lord shall renew their
strength; they shall mount up with wings like eagles;
they shall run and not be weary; they shall walk and
not faint.
Isaiah 40:31

We are so afraid that if we stop that we will lose momentum, and yet if we do not stop and wait, we will become weary and faint. We must wait until our strength is renewed once again.

The writers of Scripture frequently employ the image of hunger and thirst to illustrate deep longing for the things of God. We, too, experience a sense of fainting from our yearning. Waiting for the fulfillment of our quest causes us to hunger for our destination like weary pilgrims traveling rugged wilderness paths. This is part of God alluring us into a place where we may draw near to him, and him to us.

If you are tired and weary, surrender to his drawing you to come near. I sense that some of you reading this are even now feeling the yearning to be with him. Put this book down and yield to his longing for time with you — perfect love is about to meet with you and wash you with his clean, refreshing joy.

> *But as for me, I will look to the Lord; I will wait for*
> *the God of my salvation; my God will hear me.*
> *Micah 7:7*

The Door of Hope

It is okay to stop the frantic running and take time to just wait. The purposes of his Kingdom are not dependent upon your fast pace or your works — he is God! Be sure to accept his invitation into "waiting," even if it seems like inactivity, to allow you to stop and encounter face-to-face intimacy with him.

CHAPTER TEN

Familiarity: Thief of Intimacy

"But this is the one to whom I will look:
he who is humble and contrite in spirit
and trembles at my word."
Isaiah 66:2, ESV

"Then [Aslan] isn't safe?" said Lucy.
"Safe?" said Mr. Beaver... "Who said anything about
safe? 'Course he isn't safe. But he's good.
He's the King, I tell you."
C.S. Lewis, *The Lion, the Witch, and the Wardrobe*

I LOVE LISTENING TO WHAT God has to say to me. I love his voice and I receive such joy as I hear him speaking. Just as some people are born with a gift to sing, somehow, I was given a gift to hear. I do not take that for granted, but recently I began to wonder if I had gotten too familiar with his voice. In my familiarity with my Lord, did I begin to finish his sentences or assume conclusions to what he was saying?

We can become so familiar with hearing the voice of someone close to us that we are not actually listening. Hearing and listening can truly be two different things. We often see this in marriages. We become so familiar with our spouse that we only half-hear what is being said, our backs turned in busy activities, and we begin to assume the full meaning of what they are saying before they finish saying it. Familiarity is easy and comfortable, but it also robs us of depth and intimacy. Assumptions and carelessness are an unwanted potential result of familiarity.

When I first began hearing the voice of God and feeling his presence, I would tremble when he spoke. The awe that I experienced at the thought of the God of the universe taking time to speak to me was overwhelming and I responded attentively. I would listen, ponder, meditate, and tremble at his Word.

This reminds me of marriage; not that we tremble in awe of our spouse, but with the beginning of *first love*, the entire world stops, and our greatest pleasure is hearing the voice of our beloved. We listen intently, hanging on every word, every gesture; and every gaze is a new cause for rejoicing. As the years pass, familiarity can begin to replace the burning love that each spouse once enjoyed and embraced. Couples can begin assuming they know every move and every look, and what those gestures or expressions mean. This can create a bad habit of withholding honor and respect they once shared. Familiarity creates a carelessness and a lack of consideration for each other, which can lead to division. Familiarity that becomes lazy presumption lacks honor, intimacy, and humility.

What if the look on your spouse's face does not mean what you assumed?   If we do not stop, ask questions, and listen for answers then we will merely "hear what we hear" through our assumptions. This is a risk and reality in any long-time relationship.

Familiarity can be a thief of intimacy. Is it possible that we do this with God? As we find our true home in his goodness and love, we are freed to be more completely our true selves. Home, after all, is the place you can rest and "be yourself." But it is not an excuse to become careless about intimacy and honor.

Recently I have had a fresh wave of the fear of the Lord come upon me to break me out of familiarity with him. I had become content with the awareness of his voice, and found myself settling for life in the shallows rather than longing to launch out into the unending ocean of his love and holiness. I realized I must commune with him in the depths of intimacy and covenant. I am experiencing a time of being emptied of *me* to find *him* in a new and unfamiliar way. I go into the wilderness, expecting to discover a door of hope leading to renewed intimacy.

I wrestle with temptation to reach out and find something to fill my emptied places, because this season is unfamiliar and uncomfortable; *yet I feel a deep caution to remain emptied so that the fullness of Christ can have reign in me.* God is not trying to cause me pain, but rather is preparing me for the days ahead, because my familiarity and half-hearted listening will not serve me well in the future. (He is doing this with all of us in varying ways.)

I must learn to listen to God's voice while looking into his face, and remember to tremble at his beauty, majesty, power, and wisdom.

Many are experiencing a spiritual reset or personal reformation that is breaking them out of what is familiar and leading them to a place of *awe*. This is not possible through human strength or efforts, although it does require God's people to yield and trust him to finish the work he has begun in them. Sometimes it requires us to become still, to stop talking and just listen while becoming completely dependent on his grace to awaken us from the fog of familiarity. In this posture, surrender takes on an entirely new meaning. We make room for him and say like Mary, *"Be it unto me according to your word."*

Our posture is "willing and waiting" so that we do not run back to the commonplace and lose awe and wonder. You may be tempted to comfort yourself with what you knew before and how you functioned in the past, because it had become easy. When God removes the familiar it is strange and disorienting, but it is necessary so you can walk in greater authority and oneness with him when the work is complete.

In pondering this, I think of Esther. She had to leave everything familiar to her so she would be ready to meet the king. Forced to leave her childhood home, her family, her friends, and all that was familiar to her, she was not only groomed for presentation to the king, but also trained to take the position of queen so she could save her people.

Bravery and courage are not formed in the familiar comfort of what we know, but in the places of the unfamiliar and unknown.

Esther had to trust the counsel of her uncle Mordecai and entrust her life fully into the hands of the Lord. She could not act presumptuously or hastily, because her life and the lives of her people were hanging in the balance. She had to be emptied of her natural lifestyle and her "ordinary" responses so she was prepared to do this extraordinary thing that would save the entire Jewish race.

We are living in similar times and Jesus's bride is in a time of preparation, being emptied of all that is familiar and anything that would cause us to act hastily. We are being prepared to walk as the King's bride; a bride who carries authority yet yields to the counsel and timing of the Holy Spirit — *our "Mordecai."* We need to know when to act and when to wait, when to conceal and when to reveal. Carelessness and assumption will be costly if we do not learn to live in the wisdom and fear of the Lord.

The Power of Intimacy

The enemy is more afraid of love than any other thing. He knows he cannot steal or corrupt the love that God has for us, so he subtly attempts to dull our passion, enticing us to leave the beauty of first love through familiarity and carelessness.

> *Keep me near you like a seal you wear over your heart,*
> *like a signet ring you wear on your hand. Love is as*
> *strong as death. Passion is as strong as the grave. Its*
> *sparks become a flame, and it grows to become a great fire!*
> *Song of Solomon 8:6*

Satan wants to deceive the people of God and cause our hearts to turn to other loves, polluting the purity of first-love union between Christ and his people. This has historically stunted growth in individuals, and even squelched the fires of revival in nations. But the passion of God's love has defeated death and hell and is a wildfire that will consume every "lesser love" we turn our hearts toward.

We call for the wind of the Spirit to come and blow upon the sparks of love within our hearts, so that they are fanned into a great fire. Isn't it time for us to stop settling for familiar sparks and ask for the mighty winds of the Holy Spirit, driven by the passion of his love, to become a hurricane blowing upon our lives, enflaming his church?

> *Jesus comes from the flaming furnace of a raging,*
> *intimate fellowship, and there is nothing entirely "safe"*
> *here. There never has been. Jesus is the very substance*
> *of a love so full and fiery that even heaven must work*
> *to withstand the force of it.[1]*

---

1   Victoria Brooks, *Ministering to God: the Reach of the Heart* (Cedar Rapids, IA: Arrow Publications, 1995), 70.

When we read the Song of Solomon, we do not encounter a book about *familiar love*, but an ode to the pure and passionate love of a man and his beloved. It sings of raging fire, not softly glowing coals. Our hearts burn to know such love, and we can ask the Lord to blow on our coals, filling our hearts with fire again.

> *Awake, north wind! Rise up, south wind! Blow on my garden and spread its fragrance all around. Come into your garden, my love; taste its finest fruits.*
> *Song of Solomon 4:16*

His love will blow on our gardens to awaken love's fragrance. He invites us into his presence to drink of love until we are filled once again (Song of Solomon 5:1).

The Door of Hope

The love of our Bridegroom is a great mystery and adventure that we are invited into. It is like the door to a garden of delight and a furnace of fiery passion that his love has unlocked for you. You can pass through this garden door and begin to experience the tastes, the fragrance, the flame, and the passion that was created for you to experience.

CHAPTER ELEVEN

No More Picket Fences

*It's either the safe, secure life, living within the box
without enterprise or resourcefulness, or it's the risk of
initiative and faith, the road less traveled. Jesus wasn't
willing to live the contented, predictable, unremark-
able existence of a small-town carpenter...*
Luci Shaw, *The Crime of Living Cautiously*

WHEN JEFF AND I WERE first married I dreamed of
having a family with him and buying a home with a white
picket fence. My dream house was to be pale yellow with
white trim, and it would have a porch for us to sit on. We
both knew that we wanted to be in "full-time ministry," so
we went to Bible college to be trained. After college we
moved back to our hometown in Northern California and
began helping a small team plant a Vineyard church. It was
the mid-1980s and the Vineyard movement was growing
and thriving.

Living in the California wine country was a great blessing with its blue skies, green rolling hills, miles of vineyards,
and bright sunshine nearly every day. The Pacific Ocean and
redwood forests were both less than an hour's drive from
us, and we loved taking frequent trips to bask in the beauty
of the land. We were surrounded by both sides of our extended families and had an abundance of friends who had
shared years of memories with us.

Our lives were not perfect, but we were happy and we were home. These blessings provided a tiny element of stability and comfort in the intense times of darkness that I wrote about in earlier chapters.

By the year 2000, Jeff and I had passed through the emptiness of our long wilderness season and struggled through many fires of testing. Jeff was doing well at his job, our family had grown to six — plus a chocolate Lab — and everyone was healthy and secure. Ministry opportunities were opening for me as my writings had begun to be published on "The Elijah List" website[1] and it exposed me to many more opportunities and people than in years past. In 2001 we purchased our dream home. It was a newly built, pale yellow two-story house with white trim, surrounded by a white picket fence. We did not request the colors or the picket fence; it was what the contractor chose. We moved in two weeks before Christmas and it was like a dream come true.

Six months after moving into our dream home we received an unexpected phone call from a Canadian prophetic minister who, at the time, was living in British Columbia. We had never met this individual, but she was flying to California and wanted to have dinner with us. We had no idea why she wanted to meet with us, but we loved her ministry and were quite excited. During dinner she asked if we would pray about moving our family from California to British Columbia, Canada, to be part of the house of prayer that she had opened. (We later learned that she the Lord had shown her that we were the family she was supposed to ask to eventually oversee it.)

There was one catch to accepting the invitation: we would need to be there in six weeks!

---

1   https://www.elijahlist.com /index.php

Jeff and I were both completely against the idea, but we did the proper "Christian thing" and politely agreed that we would pray and ask the Lord what his desire was. Honestly, I did not want to pray; I did not want to even consider leaving our new home, our extended family, our city, and our beloved friends. We had just bought the home of our dreams and were enjoying a season of fruitfulness and blessings after years of hard work; and it was all surrounded by my picket fence.

Driving home I kept remembering that one of our dear friends — a trusted and godly advisor — had felt that we should not buy the house (although he didn't know why). It was the first time we had gone against his counsel, but after all, the house was perfect and the right color, and had my dream front porch and my picket fence. It had to be from God!

Well.

Less than twenty-four-hours after our dinner and commitment to pray about the invitation, unsolicited (and, honestly, *unwelcome*) confirmations began pouring in. I felt sick at the thought of uprooting our family and not only moving away from everything familiar that we loved, but to another country besides. However, over the next few weeks God made it abundantly clear that the invitation was from him.

I have probably never been so scared in my life. With four young children, no time to sell our home (which had a large mortgage), no visas, no financial support, and no way to work or earn money in Canada, I wondered how this could possibly be God's direction?

Our parents didn't understand. We were in the best position financially and spiritually we had ever been in, and we had just bought a home. It seemed irresponsible and impulsive — except for the realization that we could not deny God's confirmations and the inner "knowing" of his will.

Despite that, it felt so difficult. I finally had everything that we had worked so hard for, and yet just seven months after moving into my home with my picket fence, we were being asked to leave everything and everyone. And not to do some important work like feeding starving children or starting churches or building an orphanage; but as "prayer missionaries." At that time this was still a new concept for most and it was not well-supported or understood.

The Real "Picket Fence"

As the days and weeks went by, I began to realize that my fear and sorrow was so deep because I had built an invisible fence around my heart and my circumstances. The life and the home we had finally established was my childhood dream. The satisfaction I felt had too much of a hold on my heart. The Holy Spirit was purging me, desiring that I take down my "picket fence" that blocked the life he desired for me. I thought a house and a fence meant that I would be secure. This request to give up everything, even our livelihood, and to live in complete dependence on God left me keenly aware of where my securities lie. I did not mind having faith for salvation and deliverance, but even after all I had experienced of his goodness, to have faith in God as my provider and security was something I had not truly lived. He was asking me to let go of everything I relied on to give me earthly security so that I would fully trust in him. My dreams had become idols because they created a barricade between me and complete trust in God.

I finally said yes as wholeheartedly as I was able, and we embarked on the most terrifying and exciting adventure of our lives. It was only the beginning of running with God, unfenced.

I'm sure I am not the only one who has built their life around earthly securities while serving God. He wanted more than just my heart — he wanted my whole life. He wanted to show me what a good Father he is and how I can put my full trust in him for everything I need. I would love to say that my "yes" embarked me on a journey of immediately racing wildly into great freedom, but instead my journey led me on a path into another wilderness of facing my greatest fears. Would Father God be there for me, or abandon me in a strange and foreign land?

There were moments of great joy and open doors throughout those years, but my fence needed to be dismantled one picket at a time. God knew the process needed to take place for true joy and peace to come into my life.

Looking back, we now benefit from some realizations that come with hindsight. During our years in Canada, the housing recession hit America, and business in our area was dreadful. It would not have been surprising if we had lost our home. If we had been able to muddle through the hard times, in 2017 a fire swept through our city and that dream house was one of thousands of homes that burned.

What a merciful God to protect us from something that would have broken our hearts. It was far better to have willingly given these things up than face having them stripped from us. What a gracious God to deliver me from the need for picket fences when all I needed was him. He is helping me find my treasure in things that are not subject to rust or decay, but are eternal and cannot be destroyed.

God is jealous for us. He longs for us to trust him completely so that we can live in the joy and peace that only he can provide. This world always has trials and tribulations; it is filled with difficulties and things that are passing away, but the one thing that will stand forever and remain the same is our God. Psalm 46 speaks of this so eloquently.

> *God is our refuge and strength,*
> *a helper who is always found*
> *in times of trouble.*
> *Therefore we will not be afraid,*
> *though the earth trembles*
> *and the mountains topple*
> *into the depths of the seas,*
> *though its waters roar and foam*
> *and the mountains quake with its turmoil. Selah*
>
> *There is a river —*
> *its streams delight the city of God,*
> *the holy dwelling place of the Most High.*
> *God is within her; she will not be toppled.*
> *God will help her when the morning dawns.*
> *Nations rage, kingdoms topple;*
> *the earth melts when He lifts His voice.*
> *The Lord of Hosts is with us;*
> *the God of Jacob is our stronghold.*
> Psalm 46:1-7

The dismantling of our *picket fences* is a continuous process. It involves growth as we willingly yield to his work in our lives. It is hard to imagine how many things we learn to put our trust in that lengthen and fortify the fences around our hearts. Yet God is merciful and compassionate in his dealings with us, and he is faithful to deliver us. With every piece of my fence that is removed, I find I have greater freedom and I am released from strongholds that are holding me captive. As Jesus becomes my stronghold I am held above the shakings of earthly circumstances. Trials and turmoil come, but my foundation is in him, my security is eternal, therefore I am not shaken.

Like you, Jeff and I have been through many trials and challenging situations. We have faced infertility, miscarriage, betrayal, wildfires, loss of a home in an electrical fire, illnesses, and the death of family and friends. We have felt pain, and we have been comforted. We have grieved and have found joy again. We have experienced losses, but many of them have turned around to become unexpected blessings. I am grateful, because with each difficulty I faced, the Lord revealed another picket that I could ask him to remove. The more security we have in *things or in people*, the easier it is for the enemy to hurt us by attacking one of these false securities. When our security is fully in God, the enemy loses targets to strike. Of course, our Father delights in blessing us with homes, jobs, family, and friends, but they can never be our true security. Things of this life can so easily be taken; but nothing can separate us from Jesus.

> *And I am convinced that nothing can ever separate us from God's love. Neither death nor life, neither angels nor demons, neither our fears for today nor our worries about tomorrow — not even the powers of hell can separate us from God's love. No power in the sky above or in the earth below — indeed, nothing in all creation will ever be able to separate us from the love of God that is revealed in Christ Jesus our Lord.*
> *Romans 8:38-39*

When my security was in paychecks, homes, belongings, my husband, my children — or even the state of my nation — I was given over to worry about tomorrow and the burden of how to assure that nothing would take those securities from me. Yet, I had no control over these things remaining secure in my life. Would death strike? Would natural disasters come? Would wars break out?

Worry and unbelief caused me to try to gain control over my life and the things I love. But with each picket that is removed, I am set free to live in peace that gives me the promise that no matter the situation, nothing can separate me from God's love. I cannot concern myself or live in the security of things that are beyond my control. Now, I can have these blessings in my life without them controlling my decisions or becoming idols.

> *My heart is not proud, O LORD, my eyes*
> *are not haughty.*
> *I do not aspire to great things or matters*
> *too lofty for me.*
> *Surely, I have stilled and quieted my soul; like a*
> *weaned child with his mother,*
> *like a weaned child is my soul within me.*
> *O Israel, put your hope in the LORD, both now and*
> *forevermore.*
> *Psalm 131*

Our home is found in the unlimited boundaries of his love, and it is the most secure home that we will ever find. I can now say that *I have stilled and quieted my soul in the security of his love.*

The Door of Hope

The boundaries of his love are unlimited and unfenced. He is inviting you into open territories where you can run free. He is opening the gate of your picket fence, dismantling your barricades, and inviting you to live in the wondrous expanse of his love and goodness.

CHAPTER TWELVE

I Shall Not Want

*[The Good Shepherd] is the owner who delights in
His flock. For Him there is no greater reward, no
deeper satisfaction, than that of seeing His sheep contented, well fed, safe and flourishing under His care.*
Phillip Keller, A Shepherd Looks at Psalm 23

THE LORD IS MY SHEPHERD; I shall not want.

I shall not want! The love of God does not leave us
lacking or in want. Our hunger may increase for *more of
him*, but the deep and real *want* in our soul is to be satisfied ✗
in the goodness of his love. He is the deepest desire of our
hungry souls. There is no one like him and no love that will
satisfy like he does. He knows what we need more than we
do and as we surrender to him, letting him have his way in
us, we gain so much more than we let go of.

But as I wrote, it is hard to dismantle our fences; it can ✗
be frightening to leave behind what makes us secure. Often
believers struggle to surrender, but this is merely because
they have been used to feeding on the crumbs of self-effort,
instead of visiting the table laden with a feast that Jesus has
spread out for us. We look at surrender as a loss rather than
what it really is: the greatest gain we will ever experience.
So, we keep running back to old protections that only leave
us hungry. This may be the greatest battle that believers
face, yet if we would stop battling and just surrender, we ✗
would taste the fruits of victory.

We are working out our salvation through daily surrender and obedience to God's truth. Willingness to be changed is key to experiencing transformation that brings freedom and healing. God does not violate our wills, but will patiently wait for us to *be* willing before he moves. Even when the angel of the Lord visited Mary, announcing the miraculous conception of our Savior, she responded with a declaration of willingness,

> *"Be it unto me according to your word."*
> Luke 1:38

Such a simple act of surrender — but with eternal, cosmic consequences! This is one of my favorite prayers to pray: "Lord, be it unto me according to your word and your will."

It is from my will that I give God permission to do his will in me. It is also a great act of surrender, since I do not normally know what his will looks like. I am trusting him with my future and my steps. I may be surrendering something that I hold as precious, but I am saying, "I trust you with all of me. You can have it all. I hold nothing back!"

This does not mean that when his will begins to move my life in directions that frighten me or catch me off guard that I don't face another wrestle to take back my will. Often, I must wrestle down my desires in order to walk in his. This is especially true in the times that he has asked me to leave loved ones — especially my children. My greatest personal desire is to have my children and grandchildren nearby, but I have had to surrender that desire more than once. After I surrender, I must trust him that he knows what is best. I also must remember that we are called to pick up our cross and follow him — and that can involve pain.

> *Then Jesus told his disciples, "If anyone would come after me, let him deny himself and take up his cross*

and follow me. For whoever would save his life will
lose it, but whoever loses his life for my sake will find
it. For what will it profit a man if he gains the whole
world and forfeits his soul? Or what shall a man give
in return for his soul?
Matthew 16:24-26

There have been many sacrifices through the years that have involved denying myself to follow him. Yet, I know at the end of my life I will realize that not one sacrifice was a hardship, but rather a joyful honor bestowed upon me. Gaining what is temporary is not worth sacrificing that which is eternal. This is true for you as well; there is nothing you have given up, or one time you have denied yourself to follow him, that it has not produced an eternal reward.

When we follow him, we are constantly in his care. We are given what we need when we need it, as well as storing up treasure in heaven!

Recently one of our daughters and her husband left everything to follow Jesus to the other side of our nation. They left their home, friends, family, and financial security. A month after moving, COVID-19 hit our nation, and the world changed. Everything that they hoped to do was halted and opportunities they thought they had for travel we canceled. They spent over a year in what felt like a barren wasteland wondering why they had left everything, only to do nothing. Even as I write this book, they are still wondering, yet when I look at their journey, all I see is that they denied themselves, picked up their cross, and followed him. That alone is a beautiful and worthy sacrifice. I do not worry about what they accomplished, because their act of worship in releasing their "yes" resounds in heaven. It was a *"Be it unto me according to your word"* moment and it conceived something that we have yet to perceive.

> *He makes everything beautiful in its time. He has also*
> *set eternity in the human heart; yet no one can fath-*
> *om what God has done from beginning to end.*
> *Ecclesiastes 3:11*

God does not measure success the same way we measure success. Sometimes a "Yes" is measured in far greater ways than we can comprehend. There is an eternal fragrance rising from our lives as we follow him. It is of far more value than anything we can measure. From eternity's perspective, the obedient heart is never truly in lack.

I often think about the years Jeff and I spent directing a house of prayer. For hours and hours every day, we prayed, and worshiped and led others in prayer and worship. Years of sacrifice were given to prayer, although any measurable success could not be seen by man's standards or understanding. Our spirits knew that great things were being accomplished, but they may not have been for our eyes to see. When we prayed for other nations, we could not know if change was occurring, but I suspect that when we get to heaven, we will know all that transpired simply because we took the time to pour out our hearts in prayer.

I often think often that as I reflect on 2020. Men, women, and children flooded into Washington D.C. to pray, worship, and declare Jesus as King of our nation. According to the standards of men, our nation is worse off than we ever have been, and yet I know that not one prayer, one song, or one pure declaration fell to the ground unheard. Seeds were planted in the soil of our nation and in the heart of God that will bear fruit. Nothing is wasted when it is poured out on his feet.

While Jesus was in Bethany in the home of Simon the Leper, a woman came to him with an alabaster jar of very expensive perfume, which she poured on his head as he was reclining at the table.

When the disciples saw this, they were indignant. "Why this waste?" they asked. "This perfume could have been sold at a high price and the money given to the poor."

Aware of this, Jesus said to them, "Why are you bothering this woman? She has done a beautiful thing to me. The poor you will always have with you, but you will not always have me. When she poured this perfume on my body, she did it to prepare me for burial. Truly I tell you, wherever this gospel is preached throughout the world, what she has done will also be told, in memory of her."
Matthew 26:6-13

"She has done a beautiful thing to me!"

These are the words that I long to hear when I am face to face before him. There is no greater reward than knowing that I have *wasted my life* as an offering poured out over his feet. When we pour out what is most valuable to us it fills the atmosphere with a beautiful fragrance, and it is never considered a waste.

If you have tried to measure your life according to man's measurements, it may be time to reconsider your measuring stick. Declare the goodness of your Shepherd who leads you as you declare "I shall not want." You have done things in the secret place that can only be measured by the standards of heaven. At the end of our lives the only waste will be that which we held back. Everything poured out will be counted as gain.

The Door of Hope

We open the door of our will to God through our willingness. We have been given freedom that God will not violate. He waits patiently at the door of our will when asking anything of us. That door, when yielded to his will, opens up the greatest adventure and the wildest of loves that we will ever experience. It will also cause us to face our fears and let go of control. This surrender ushers in satisfaction, healing, abundance, and freedom that we can only experience through his faithfulness and goodness. The world opens doors that leave us wanting, but our Shepherd is the door that causes us to walk into joy and favor, declaring boldly "I shall not want" (I lack nothing).

CHAPTER THIRTEEN

The Winter is Over

"Arise, my love, my beautiful one, and come away,
for behold, the winter is past; the rain is over and gone.
The flowers appear on the earth,
the time of singing has come...
Song of Solomon 2:10-12

THE WILDERNESS SEASONS IN OUR lives are just that
— *seasons.* They vary in length, and can feel like a dark, frigid winter that will never end, but one day there is a realization that *"The winter is over."* Every wilderness season I have gone through, I have held onto hope that the season would surely end and that growth and beauty would emerge. Just as God found it was good to give the earth a winter season every year, so he sees it is fitting to allow winter to come upon our lives as well. In these seasons, growth happens underground, in the unseen places. Autumn sheds the earth of old growth and winter prepares the fresh growth that will appear in spring. We wish it could be different, but you cannot have spring without a winter. It is a necessary process in our lives just as much as on the earth. If you only look with eyes of the flesh, you will miss the hidden wonders happening in the unseen places. Even a butterfly is transformed from a caterpillar in a dark, hidden place. A baby is knit together in secret, in the womb of its mother.

Throughout this book, I have shared how I experience

more growth and transformation in the wilderness than at any other time. The journey can be accompanied by pain, but it produces the character of Jesus in a way no other season can. Even in the darkness, you can rejoice, hoping that soon your spring will appear and what the pain has produced will appear as a great transformation.

> *The fig tree ripens its figs,*
> *and the vines are in blossom;*
> *they give forth fragrance.*
> *Arise, my love, my beautiful one,*
> *and come away.*
> *O my dove, in the clefts of the rock,*
> *in the crannies of the cliff,*
> *let me see your face,*
> *let me hear your voice,*
> *for your voice is sweet,*
> *and your face is lovely.*
> *Catch the foxes for us,*
> *the little foxes*
> *that spoil the vineyards,*
> *for our vineyards are in blossom."*
> Song of Solomon 2:13-15

"*Catch the little foxes that spoil the vineyards…*" There are so many "little foxes" that the enemy sends into the vineyard of our lives. They come to spoil the vineyards and to destroy the tender blossoms. Often the moment spring appears in our lives, little foxes run in to upset the blossoms before our true fruit appears. Yet, I have found that the character produced in the winter season enables us to identify and catch these foxes before they cause damage to the fruit that will soon appear upon the branches of our lives.

Finding Foxes

What are these little foxes and how can we identify them? They can come in many forms, but their goal is to spoil what was formed in your winter season before it bears fruit: regret, temptation, distraction…the list is long.

A story from my husband's life (shared with his permission) is a good illustration.

Jeff has always been a man who honors me with such love and a servant's heart. From the day we met, he showed me honor in all that he did. From opening my car door (which he still does thirty-eight years on) to serving me with great self-sacrifice — his posture toward me is always honor. Even during the three years of my deep depression when we were young, he covered me and constantly was changing my filthy garments and clothing me with purity and honor. He believed the Lord would complete the work that he had begun in me and so he honored me and rebuked the enemy that would accuse me. I believe it is because of his honor and the honor of some dear friends, that I could come through that time and be restored to sitting in places of honor and dignity.

Fifteen years after my *dark night of the soul,* my precious husband went through a traumatic time that sought to steal his honor and clothe him with shame. We had just returned home from four years of ministry in another country. Jeff returned to his old job in the marketplace because he frankly could not think of anything else he could do. All his training was in ministry and in one area of business, but no ministry doors were opening in the States for us, and no business opportunities either. Even though he thought he had left it for good years earlier, he returned to the company he had worked for prior to our time in Canada. Jeff had spent many years in this line of work, but it did not really "fit" his talents or personality. He was financially successful, but the effort had always been a deep drain on him emotionally and spiritually.

The U.S. was in the beginning phases of the deep economic recession and housing crisis, which deepened as we entered 2008. We quickly realized that the success Jeff had previously known was not possible. The pressure on him was extraordinary, and he could not bring in the finances that we needed. Living in California was expensive, and business opportunities were scarce.

Approximately six months after moving, we came home one day to find our home on fire — the result of an electrical problem. We lost almost everything. Then our teenaged children came under strange attacks and temptations from the enemy. Our oldest daughter, whom we had adopted, who was such a gift to us, walked away from the Lord. Jeff and I felt as though the enemy had come and was hitting us on every side.

We had spent years directing a house of prayer and walking with believers in other nations to see them restored to God's original intent, but as soon as we moved back home, it was as if all hell was unleashed against us. Even some of our dearest relationships were attacked as we lost friends through misunderstandings that caused ruptures which appeared irreparable.

After few years of this, I noticed that Jeff was worn down and deeply discouraged. His personality changed from loving and attentive to me and his children, to distant and defensive. I was still writing for prophetic publications, as well as traveling for ministry, but what was happening with Jeff was so painful and disorienting that I considered stopping.

I was losing sight of who he had been; the kind and loving man I married was angry, secretive, and unpredictable. This man who had led worship and prayer throughout other nations was becoming unrecognizable. I had no idea what to do. I didn't feel that I had anyone to turn to so I would cry myself to sleep, begging God to help us. I wanted my husband back, my family back, and the favor of the Lord back.

Finally, one January night, I found Jeff unconscious and unresponsive from an overdose of alcohol and had to call 911. I had never seen him drunk, let alone unconscious from alcohol. He was rushed to the hospital in an ambulance, and I followed in shock and disbelief. Truly, I did not recognize my life any longer. This night led to the awareness that my precious husband had fallen into alcoholism.

He was drinking daily, and he hid it for a long time by consuming enough that he was continually in a state of low-level intoxication, but still able to function. Late that night, however, while everyone in the house was asleep, he drank until he was unresponsive. I woke up in the middle of the night, saw he wasn't in bed, went downstairs to check on him, and discovered what had happened. Up to that point I had been totally unaware of what was going on, and I was devastated.

But during this time we experienced a personal "Zechariah 3" moment.[1] God was present to change my husband's filthy garments and to rebuke the enemy. He sent friends — even ministry leaders and partners — to cover us and clothe us with the purity of love and honor. Our house filled with family and friends who came to hold us, love us, and pray

---

1   The prophet Zechariah's powerful vision of God stripping Joshua the high priest of filthy garments, and clothing him in pure priestly raiment, is in Zechariah 3:1-7.

over us. Not one person brought shame or accusation, but all came to restore honor and dignity to our family.

Even our children acted with such honor toward their dad that it healed deep places within his soul. The night he came home from the hospital, he was still going through withdrawals, and the shame he felt was overwhelming. Our children gathered in our bedroom and decided that they would stay with him all night. They turned on his favorite family movies and laid on blankets and pillows in our room so that he knew he was not alone.

They loved him with such honor that he never took another drink.

I watched God, friends, and our children represent God to him with honor and beauty. I genuinely believe that it was the honor that we showed him that restored him so quickly and thoroughly. Within a year our finances, our family, and even our ministry had been restored. Most of all, our hearts were restored to a place of dignity and honor.[2]

Three years after Jeff's victory and restoration, he wrote a poignant article about a "little fox" that snuck in amid his restorative spring season, attempting to steal the blossoms that were just about to produce a huge harvest of fruit in his life. I share what he wrote because I believe it will bless you and show you how to catch those little foxes.

His particular little foxes were *guilt* and *unbelief*.

---

2 Jeff's recounting of part of his story is at: https://te-homblog.wordpress.com/2017/01/05/ashes-to-beauty/

"Nothing is Wasted " by Jeffrey Pelton[3]
February 2017

RECENTLY, I WROTE OF A VERY DARK SEASON in my life. I had been a Christian for decades and had served in leadership in various ministries and churches. But all that time, I carried unhealed hurt that, in my self-sufficiency, I felt I could ignore. I also never addressed my subtle but persistent unbelief in God's goodness and love for me personally. I was always able to connect with his heart for others — especially the innocent and neglected — but somehow it did not transfer over to an ongoing encounter of his love and favor in my personal experience.

I think many believers can relate. We know the Lord loves us — at least, we give lip service to that truth. But in the deepest recesses of our souls, when we lie awake in the middle of the night, we find ourselves appalled and frightened by the darkness we feel is still within us.

Guilt can be a merciless and unmovable monster, screeching condemnation and clawing at our sensitive conscience. We feel overwhelmed and ashamed by weakness and failure. If we fail to recognize the incalculable pardon and mercy we have received from Jesus' sacrifice, we will cower before its onslaught, aghast at the thought that God must be angry and disgusted with us, and frantic with fear that other people might discover what we are really like. Like someone in the bullseye of a tornado's path, we are whirled ruthlessly in a maelstrom of questions:

---

3   https://tehomblog.wordpress.com/2017/02/24/nothing-is-wasted/

Why aren't I obeying/praying/reading Scripture/ministering as I should?

Why don't I love God more?

Why do I keep sinning the way I do?

Will I ever stop failing?

Has the Lord really forgiven me.......?

A few mornings ago, as I prayed, my thoughts stumbled down that ugly path as I began to recall many instances of dreadful failure from my "dark night of the soul." I had been forgiven by God and man, but I still found myself sick at heart with regret about the wasted years of sin and unfaithfulness. I felt I personified Jeremiah's words: *The heart is deceitful above all things, and desperately wicked* (Jeremiah 17:9). Surely my actions had proven that to everyone.

Several months ago, the Holy Spirit powerfully spoke to me the promise of Joel 2:25: *I will restore to you the years that the swarming locust has eaten, the crawling locust, the consuming locust, and the chewing locust.* Although I believe the promise, as I prayed it did not seem to have much reality in light of the parade of wretchedness reminding me of the incredible defeat in my life. I felt disqualified from any promise or fullness of what my life could have been as I knelt, ashamed and dejected.

Suddenly, I felt as if I was transported to the feet of Jesus, much like the woman caught in adultery in John chapter eight. I sensed Jesus asking me: "Where are those accusers of yours? Has no one condemned you?"

In an instant I realized the gracious truth of Romans 8:1 (*There is therefore now no condemnation to those who are in Christ Jesus!*) as I lifted my head and replied: "No one, Lord."

He said, "Neither do I condemn you; go and sin no more."

As his words washed over me, I was aware of the presence of the Holy Spirit and I was conscious of the awe-inspiring I AM overseeing the timeline of my life. I couldn't see the details — my life did not flash before me — but somehow, I knew at that moment HE examined it all, reviewing and sifting all the evidence.

And in that awareness, I heard his quiet, powerful voice: "Son, nothing is wasted."

I was overcome as I realized that even in my weakest, darkest moments, he understood, with utter perfection, every desire and motivation of my heart. He was intimately aware of every howl of pain when I screamed and cursed in anger instead of crying out in humble brokenness. He saw every wicked craving that sprouted and flourished like twisted vines, choking my true desire to be satisfied in him. He recognized that even as I attempted to numb myself so I would not feel the inferno of torment and despair that I carried because of my sin, I was crying silently with desperate hope I might find a place of true repentance.

God himself presides as Refiner's Fire (Malachi 3) over each moment of our existence. As we humble ourselves in the fear of the Lord, he hears us and writes in his book of remembrance. He declares over us that we are his. In his mercy he reaches into our lives and extracts the precious from the worthless (Jeremiah 15:19).

You may feel that you have failed, perhaps wretchedly and repeatedly, as I did. But the Father has a different viewpoint. You may believe you have been unfaithful, you have sinned, you have spurned his love and grace, you have done things you should not have, you have not done what you ought. But God doesn't look at outward appearances; he reads the heart. He is able to discern and nurture the true and precious promise of life he has placed within you. He is able to take even your failures and your weaknesses and extract what is precious.

Do not be afraid to run to your Father, who knows you intimately and perfectly (Psalm 139).

Even though you may only see worthlessness and sin from the failures of your life, he perceives every pure seed of love and faithfulness. He has not forgotten every wavering resolution to obey him. He remembers it all, and from the ashes of failure he extracts what is precious, purifies it, and creates radiant jewels for his eternal glory within you.

Nothing of value, no matter how seemingly insignificant, is forgotten.

Nothing is wasted.

Maybe your winter season has not looked like dormancy and underground growth. Maybe you have reacted by kicking and screaming. Sin may have grown upon the bare limbs of your life, threatening to choke out any possibility of you bearing fruit or carrying his glory again. And it may have been years rather than months, just as both my husband's ✻ and my dark nights of the soul lasted three years.

As Jeffrey so beautifully shared, nothing is wasted. When we surrendered, suddenly blossoms appeared, and our lives produced more fruit than we ever dreamed possible. We learned how to identify the foxes of shame, guilt, and despair — chasing them out with the testimony of how Jesus saved our lives. Our growth and deliverance took place quietly, in unseen depths of our souls, even as our sin and shame appeared to have been laid bare for all who knew us to see. But what mercy and what kindness poured over our ✻ lives in those seasons. He saw beyond the pain and beyond the sin to the anguish in our hearts that cried out for him to ✻ rescue and save us. And he did!

In the many years we have journeyed in freedom since those times, God has used our stories to help and give hope to others caught in the grip of shame or sin. For both of us, our sin of unbelief regarding the depths of his love, grace, and mercy was far greater than the sins of self-harm or alcoholism — those were merely the mechanisms we used to cope with our lack of trust. Just like when the Lord walked into the bathroom to hold my hair back, or when he prompted our children gather around their dad until he knew he had not lost them — this is how much he loves us. These are the moments that the tender buds of spring signal that life has not been lost and a door of hope is once again standing before us to cross through.

No matter where you are or what you've done — he can redeem it, rewrite it, and turn it into beauty. He surely does make beauty from ashes.

The Spirit of the Sovereign Lord is on me,
because the Lord has anointed me

to proclaim good news to the poor.
He has sent me to bind up the brokenhearted,
to proclaim freedom for the captives
and release from darkness for the prisoners,
to proclaim the year of the LORD's favor
and the day of vengeance of our God,
to comfort all who mourn,
and provide for those who grieve in Zion—
to bestow on them a crown of beauty
instead of ashes,
the oil of joy
instead of mourning,
and a garment of praise
instead of a spirit of despair.
They will be called oaks of righteousness,
a planting of the LORD
for the display of his splendor.

They will rebuild the ancient ruins
and restore the places long devastated;
they will renew the ruined cities
that have been devastated for generations.
Strangers will shepherd your flocks;
foreigners will work your fields and vineyards.
And you will be called priests of the LORD,
you will be named ministers of our God.
You will feed on the wealth of nations,
and in their riches you will boast.

Instead of your shame
you will receive a double portion,
and instead of disgrace
you will rejoice in your inheritance.

And so you will inherit a double portion in your land,
and everlasting joy will be yours.

"For I, the LORD, love justice;
I hate robbery and wrongdoing.
In my faithfulness I will reward my people
and make an everlasting covenant with them.
Their descendants will be known among the nations
and their offspring among the peoples.
All who see them will acknowledge
that they are a people the LORD has blessed."

I delight greatly in the LORD;
my soul rejoices in my God.
For he has clothed me with garments of salvation
and arrayed me in a robe of his righteousness,
as a bridegroom adorns his head like a priest,
and as a bride adorns herself with her jewels.
For as the soil makes the sprout come up
and a garden causes seeds to grow,
so the Sovereign LORD will make righteousness
and praise spring up before all nations.
Isaiah 61

The Door of Hope

I have stated it many times in this book: When we find ourselves wandering through the Valley of Trouble, there is always a door into hope, redeeming the promises God placed in our hearts that we feared lost in the cold darkness. He transforms us as we trust the Holy Spirit to have his way in us during these times. I recently had a vision of a little girl, wrapped in filthy rags, who clutched a tattered and filthy rag doll as she stumbled in a lonely wilderness. But as she walked, she was gradually cleansed and transformed. She arrived at a doorway opening onto a path that led out of the wilderness, and as she hesitated, I saw Jesus come to carry her over the threshold. She was now clothed in a shimmering white dress, and even her little rag doll was an exquisite new china doll. She was no longer in rags, and even what she had carried into the wilderness had been transformed.

Nothing was wasted; everything was made new.

CHAPTER FOURTEEN

Open Up!

The Lord is still asking, "Whom shall I send?" and
we can answer, "Here I am. Send me."
Then watch what happens.

IMAGINE SOMEONE JOURNEYING through the Valley of Trouble, and on reaching a door opening to a vast land of promise, the person sits down, thinking *Well, I guess all my hope was in vain.*

To pass through a door, first you have to open it.

Every home has a front door for their guests to enter, but family often enters through a back door — a door for those who live there. I have discovered many doors in my Father's house. Initially, there was a front door I was invited to pass through to visit and explore. After salvation I was given a key so I could dwell in the house of the Lord. As the years have passed, I have discovered many doors that I am invited to open. There are doors of opportunity, doors of mysteries revealed (revelation doors), doors of intimacy, and doors to elevators that take us to new heights. Throughout Scripture, we read about many types of doors, including Jesus, who is the door that his sheep enter through.

When I was about four years old, I had a reoccurring experience that would always frighten me. Night after night I would lay in bed (with the light on because I feared the dark) and I would see the opposite wall appear to recede farther and farther away from me. It would become a long hallway with many doors on either side. I would be pulled down this hallway, but I was too frightened to open any of the doors in it. Stuck in this long, narrow hallway, I was pulled further away from the safety of my bed.

I don't know if this was a reoccurring dream, a child's vivid imagination, or a spiritual occurrence; I just know that I would often find myself stuck in this hallway filled with closed doors I could not open. After I gave my life to Christ, it was as though I returned to that never-ending hallway and watched door after door open for me. Each door opened a new experience, an adventure with vivid color and dreams fulfilled. It was as if my life before Jesus was limited to walking a never-ending corridor with doors that would not open for me. I was stuck in a lonely, long hallway with nowhere else to go, no dreams to dream, and no color to be seen.

We all have seasons of transition that might feel like that hallway of doors, but as sons and daughters of God we are offered a door of hope that opens to new vistas we never could have imagined. I have been amazed where some of these doors have led me. There have been doors opened to fulfillment of personal dreams, and to opportunities that I never dreamed possible. Some of those doors have taken me to places like Germany, Japan, and Canada, as well as a season of living in the Washington D.C. region. I have made many friends who are workers in this great harvest throughout the world — from the Arctic to Egypt — from Israel to Brazil. What a colorful and adventurous life we live from the doors that the Lord opens for us.

Some of you reading this may have experienced similar things as you yielded to the Lord's plans for your life. If you have not, and you are now thinking, "Hey, what about me?"— just ask! God has amazing plans for his children;

plans beyond what you can ask or imagine. Most of what I have done, I had not even imagined doing, so I did not consider asking. But God encourages us to believe him!

> Now to him who is able to do immeasurably more than all we ask or imagine, according to his power that is at work within us, to him be glory in the church and in Christ Jesus throughout all generations, for ever and ever! Amen.
> Ephesians 3:20-21

The enemy wants us to remain in the hallway with closed doors and nowhere to go. Jesus is the open door that leads to many doors, and his plans are to always be opening new doors for you to walk through. His doors open to great purposes for his kingdom as well as wonderful pleasures. Wherever he has placed you, God will open doors that no man, or enemy, can shut.

> What he opens no one can shut, and what he shuts no one can open. I know your deeds. See, I have placed before you an open door that no one can shut. I know that you have little strength, yet you have kept my word and have not denied my name.
> Revelation 3:7-8

During my time of healing, before we moved to Canada, while my children were young and I had all the responsibilities and busy life of a mom, I began reaching out in our city to find open doors in people's hearts. I would ask the Holy Spirit to lead me to unlocked doors within the hearts of men and women seeking salvation.

I had attended a women's conference with a dear friend,

and one session during the weekend deeply impacted me. The preacher's message revolved around a passage from Isaiah 6:

> *Then I heard the Lord asking, "Whom should I send*
> *as a messenger to this people? Who will go for us?" I*
> *said, "Here I am. Send me."*
> *Isaiah 6:8*

I responded to the Holy Spirit's prompting and said "Yes, Lord. Here I am; send me. I will be your messenger."

One short prayer in one holy moment opened a door that changed my life. Suddenly, my regular tasks became a continual opportunity to share the goodness of God with people I encountered. Each week I would experience divine appointments that would leave me in awe at the beauty and love of God. God was listening to the desires and longings of people in our city and he would look for someone who had opened the door of their heart to go on his behalf. I was always thrilled when he would pick me. My children were young and I did not have the ability to travel, but I did not need to go to another country; the hungry and needy were right in my city, waiting for someone to go to them.

The Lord is still asking, "Whom shall I send?" and we can answer by saying, "Here I am. Send me." Then watch what happens.

I believe if we could see what God sees, we would realize that there are spiritual doors all around us each day that we could go through. So often we choose to remain in the hallway of mediocrity, merely putting one foot in front of the other, not recognizing that the doors we pass are there for us to walk through. We get so familiar with the "hallway" that we do not even notice the doors any longer. Or we believe that the doors are only for certain *gifted* people. Not true! They are for anyone willing to say, *"Here I am."*

Jesus's disciples were ordinary men. Fishermen, tax collectors, doctors, and tent makers. They were pulled straight from their fishing boats and ordinary lives. They did not go to Bible college or seminary — they merely sat at the feet of Jesus to learn and walked beside him as he went out. Jesus was their master, teacher, and open door.

As believers, his Spirit now lives within us and we too can sit at his feet and walk with him. He is our master, teacher, and open door. You are qualified because you have the same Spirit in you who walked with Jesus on earth. The Lord did not force any of his disciples — he invited them to leave the life they knew to come and follow him. The same is true today. We can say "yes" to his invitation or we can stay in the hallway, walking past doors that lead to someone who needs the Master's touch.

I am not suggesting that every person reading this book leave their jobs to become an evangelist. I am saying that you can say "Here I am" and he will show you a door that needs to be opened. He is just looking for those who will respond to his invitation to follow. When doors began opening for me, I was busy with young children, helping to run a private school, working part-time at a job, running a household, and helping to pastor a church. When I could not go, I found that the Lord would bring the doors to where I was.

Even during COVID-19 and all the shutdowns, I can reach people in so many ways. God is creative and knows where we are and how to work within our circumstances. When we open the door of our hearts to him, he opens doors of opportunity to us.

As I was writing this chapter, I was taken into a vision of

an open door that I believe will encourage you. This vision is for the days ahead, when the world will become like one large open door for his Spirit and salvation to come to the masses.

"The Open Door"

IN MY VISION I SAW the month of April on a calendar before me. A wind blew upon this calendar page and as the wind touched it, the page suddenly became an open door. This open door led into a beautiful fragrant garden that brought an immediate sense of hope and joy to my soul. The Latin meaning for the name April means, *Open up*. God had my attention.

As this April door blew open, I heard the verse from Song of Solomon 4:16,

Awake, north wind! Rise up, south wind! Blow on my garden and spread its fragrance all around. Come into your garden, my love; taste its finest fruits.

I saw the wind as *the breath of God, the Ruach* — as his breath was released upon his sons and daughters—new life, even resurrection life, came upon them. A fragrance, like a garden in full bloom, came forth from them that filled the earth. I saw each son and daughter take their place as a part of this garden that was filled with fragrant blossoms and sweet fruits. The fragrance went beyond the garden into the whole world.

When I saw this, I became aware that most of the world had lost their sense of smell and their sense of taste (just like what happens when many people contract COVID-19). They had lost their sense of smell and taste for God. The Lord created every man and woman with the senses to seek after him, but the thief had stolen their senses. Yet, when the wind blew this door open, not only did God's children come into full bloom but the fragrance and taste of the Lord came upon their lives and it began to awaken the senses of those who had lost their senses. I saw prodigals returning as they *"came to their senses."* I saw "seekers" suddenly finding the scent of what they were seeking. They were like dogs who had been following a scent but had lost it and were walking in circles trying to find it again— but suddenly they found the scent and it led them to salvation.

I saw many of God's sons and daughters longing for passion and purpose. When this wind blew, it awakened them like a wind coming upon a smoldering ember that was extremely near to being extinguished. This wind caused it to turn bright amber in color with a burning glow of his love and presence. Then the dry and barren place that they had been existing in caught fire and they burned with passion and purpose to carry his glory, his fragrance and his fire. They became a great fire that could not be contained.

Fragrance, fruit, and fire[1] will mark the days ahead as we walk through the open door named April. The breath (wind) of God will sovereignly open this door and it will be like when the stone was rolled away from the tomb of our Savior. His *ekklesia*[2] will come forth with fragrance, fruitfulness, and great fire. Resurrection power will be upon us once again.

Where much of the world viewed the church as a tomb with a stone blocking its entrance — they will be-

---

1   See chapter 10.

2   A people called out from the world and unto God; church.

gin to see an open door that is releasing the scent that they have longed for and they will find the treasure that they have been searching for. No longer will it be a place that represents dead works, but it will be a garden of life full of the choicest fruits and a fire that will ignite passion and purpose within them. Even tongues of fire will fall once again, and salvation will fall upon people as they merely walk into the fragrant atmosphere.

Altars will be so full in the days to come that his people will create altars in barns, tents, fields, farms, parking lots and even in theaters. Living rooms will become altars where salvation comes to the young and the old. Even front yards will become churches where entire neighborhoods are transformed by the fire falling upon them.

> *"Not by power, not by might but by my Spirit" says*
> *the Lord.*
> Zechariah 4:6

Begin to call for the wind of the Spirit to blow! Call for the fire of the Spirit to fall and to ignite! Call for the Spirit and the bride to say, "Come!"

> *The Spirit and the bride say, "Come." Let anyone*
> *who hears this say, "Come." Let anyone who is*
> *thirsty come. Let anyone who desires drink freely*
> *from the water of life.*
> Revelation 22:17

Come, north wind! Rise up, south wind! Blow on my garden and spread its fragrance all around! *Do you hear him calling to you — "Open Up!"*

The Door of Hope

Your amazing Savior holds the key to open doors before you. Doors that lead to opportunities beyond your ability to ask or imagine as well as doors that lead to those who are seeking truth. No believer should be experiencing locked door after locked door. If this has been your experience, Jesus holds the key to open doors that no man can shut and shut doors that no man can open. More than anything else, open up the door of your heart and let him blow on your garden.

CHAPTER FIFTEEN

Becoming Home

"Heaven is my throne, and the earth is my footstool.
Where is the house you will build for me? Where will
my resting place be?"
Isaiah 66:1

WHAT DOES GOD MEAN WHEN he says he is looking
for a resting place? As Solomon prayed, "Will God indeed
dwell on the earth? Behold, heaven and the highest heaven
cannot contain you; how much less this house that I have
built!" (1 Kings 8:27, ESV). And Stephen, in his magnif-
icent preaching before his martyrdom, proclaimed "… the
Most High does not dwell in houses made by hands…"
(Acts 7:48, ESV). So if God is not looking for timeshares
or temples, where is this "place" for him to rest?

And since we are created in God's image, could our
longing to find home come from him?

> *"Don't let your hearts be troubled. Trust in God,*
> *and trust also in me. There is more than enough*
> *room in my Father's home. If this were not so, would*
> *I have told you that I am going to prepare a place for*
> *you? When everything is ready, I will come and get*
> *you, so that you will always be with me where I am."*
> *John 14:1-3*

The Holy Spirit is the full representation of the Father and the Son and he acts in perfect unity with the other two members of the Godhead. Jesus came to restore humanity to his Father, and the Spirit comes and makes his home in every believer, so that the power of God's love will continue to walk the earth through us. He longs to bring everyone to the knowledge of salvation through Christ. Even as we find our home in the refuge of Christ, so he is looking for a home within those who love him and walk with him.

> *Jesus replied, "Anyone who loves me will obey my teaching. My Father will love them, and we will come to them and make our home with them."*
> *John 14:23*

Notice that this verse says, "*our home.*" We know that the Father, Son, and Holy Spirit are one. When the Holy Spirit came to live within us, we have the love of God poured out within us. When Jesus said that it was better for him to leave this world so the Advocate could come, we must remember that Jesus was the representation of the Father; he ascended back to the Father, his Spirit descended to dwell within us, and we were given the miracle of having the *Three-in-One* making a home within us collectively and individually.

> *"My prayer is not for them alone. I pray also for those who will believe in me through their message, that all of them may be one, Father, just as you are in me and I am in you. May they also be in us so that the world may believe that you have sent me. I have given them the glory that you gave me, that they may be one as we are one— I in them and you in me—so that they may be brought to complete unity. Then the world will*

know that you sent me and have loved them even as
you have loved me.
John 17:20-23

It is when the Spirit finds his home in us that we become the message of Jesus and carriers of his Father's love. John 17 records Jesus's last prayer before going to the cross. I love that he says, "I have given them the glory that you gave me, that they may be one as we are one." This is how we experience unity and how the world will know that the Father sent his Son for them. The love of the Father, fully known by the Son, now resides in us through his Spirit. What a priceless gift to those who ask Jesus to live in their hearts! There is nothing better than experiencing the love that changes everything — it is the glory that Jesus walked with. If only we could even begin to grasp the height and depth and breadth of his love, it would change everything. Just a taste of it satisfies a lifetime of longing. I am reminded once again of the verse in 1 Corinthians 2:9-10 that tells us, "The Spirit searches all things, even the deep things of God."

The Spirit has searched out the depths of the love of God and now he lives in us radiating the depths of that love. It is available for us day and night, and it is available to every person we encounter. We carry his glory and can release his glory wherever we go. He is looking for people who are ready to receive his love. Often, they don't know they are ready — sometimes they don't realize they are even looking! — but the Spirit of God knows. This truth always leaves me awestruck. He knows us better than we know ourselves and even before he resides in us, he knows when we are ready. His pursuit of us is one of the most beautiful things that I have ever encountered. What love!

*This is love: He loved us long before we loved him. It was
his love, not ours. He proved it by sending his Son to be
the pleasing sacrificial offering to take away our sins.*
1 John 4:10

He pursued us before we were ever even born. This is love. Jesus died for us, providing the way for salvation and life with him before we knew we needed a way. I am continually overwhelmed by this truth.

Our youngest daughter and her husband have been trying to start a family for almost ten years without success, and I watch them month after month, year after year, love a child that they have never met. They have prepared for this child, buying little outfits and blankets, and filling their hearts with love and dreams for this child that has yet to be conceived.

Jeff and I also faced many years of not being able to conceive and I keenly remember treasuring deep love in my heart for our children whom we had never met or held. I would weep with deep, aching longing for them, and now I have watched my daughter do the same thing. We waited less than a decade for our first child; our Father has waited for his sons and daughters, whom he created, to receive his arms of love for thousands of years — since the foundation of the world. Even before creation, he knew you and loved you.

*Even before he made the world, God loved us and chose
us in Christ to be holy and without fault in his eyes.*
Ephesians 1:4

When Jeff and I were trying to start a family, a door opened for us to adopt a baby girl. The process of getting her was far more difficult than we could have imagined, but

I will never forget the absolute joy and fulfillment we experienced the day we held her for the first time. She was eleven months old, and we must have kissed every inch of her: every toe and finger; the top of her little head; her forehead; her cheeks. We ran our fingers through her beautiful curls and soaked them with tears as we took in her beauty.

I did not sleep our first night with her. Jeff and I laid her in bed between us and I just stared at her for hours by the light of the moon. Then, much to my surprise and utter joy, in the middle of the night she turned toward me and put her tiny hand on my face and in a little voice said, "Mommy."

She had been waiting for us too. I held her for hours, my tears of joy bathing her with love. Though we had never seen each other before that day, our hearts had been knit together through hope and longing.

I am reminded of this often when I think of how God must feel when pursuing us. He knows our hearts were created to find home in his love. When we finally become aware of his first touch, our hearts cry, "*Daddy.*" How often his tears must bathe us as we sleep! If he knows the number of hairs upon our heads, then we understand he looks upon us the way I treasured our new baby girl. He is overwhelmed with love for every part of who you are. As I stared at our daughter through the eyes of love, I could see no flaw in her — to Jeff and me, she was perfect. Our Father has that heart for us. He longs for every person to find their true identity and their home in him as he, in turn, finds his home in them.

We were created to be the recipients of unconditional love. We thrive when we experience God's love in oneness with him and unity with one another. The experience of his agape love removes all striving, all competition, and all disunity. We become complete and lack nothing, so we do not have to compete with each other out of jealousy.

When our youngest daughter was in kindergarten, she was very possessive of me. I volunteered each week to help in her class when they did art assignments. She would be so excited for me to show up, and yet not long after I'd arrive, she would be in tears because she did not like me giving attention to the other kids. She didn't like it when the other children gave me a hug or asked for my attention. Her eyes would well up with big tears as she whispered to me, "You're my mommy, not theirs." She did not understand at that tender age how incredibly deep was my love for her. I tried to explain to her that no one could steal the love and affection I had for her, so she didn't need to cry or experience pangs of jealousy, because nothing could separate my love from her.

I think of this when I see jostling for attention or position among members of the body of Christ. I think of my little girl crying rather than enjoying my presence there with her. I wonder why we do not realize the incomprehensible richness of his love for us — a love that began before the foundations of the earth. Each of us receive the fullness of God's love inside us, so there is no need to compete for his love or attention.

As we come into this understanding, we can allow the prayer of Jesus in John 17 to be made manifest in us. We will come into oneness with him, and we will also allow unity and oneness to formed with our brothers and sisters in Christ. One God, one body, one home — then the world will know!

the Door of Hope

Our hearts are a door the Lord knocks on. He longs to enter and dwell within us, and he invites us to live in him. He has prepared a home for us, and he looks for a home in us as well, drawing us into the oneness that the Father, Son, and Holy Spirit share. He invites us to become a part of his glory — the glory available for every son and daughter of God. This glory and unity reveal to the world that the Father sent Jesus as our Messiah. Holy union is a revelation that opens the eyes of the world to see a love that is pure and genuinely inclusive. We become a demonstration of the Father's love, inviting his wayward sons and daughters to come home.

CHAPTER SIXTEEN

You're Home

*"Behold, the tabernacle of God is with men, and He
will dwell with them, and they shall be His people.
God Himself will be with them and be their God.
And God will wipe away every tear from their eyes;
there shall be no more death, nor sorrow, nor crying.
There shall be no more pain, for the former things
have passed away."*
Revelation 21:3-4, NKJV

I BEGAN WRITING THIS BOOK as a way to process the agony I felt over my brother's death in the opening days of 2021. I had been brutally thrust out of an extended season of joy and blessings into a deep wilderness of grief and pain.

I wrote in chapter three that the morning of December 31, 2020, I received a call from my only brother and his wife asking us for prayer. They had both tested positive for COVID-19 two weeks previously, and although Lisa had recovered fully, Bob (Bobby to me) was getting worse each day. He could barely talk on the call, except to gasp out his request that we pray. Our family gathered around the phone and we took turns praying for him. By nature, he was always energetic and overflowing with enthusiasm, but only a few months earlier he had finished his last round of chemotherapy for lymphoma.

He had been declared cancer-free and we all rejoiced at this victory, but we were also aware that his immune system could be vulnerable to the effects of the virus.

After our phone call, Lisa decided to take Bob to the emergency room to see if doctors could help with his breathing. The hospital admitted him but would not let family into the ER or the hospital with him because of restrictions surrounding the pandemic. The first two days he seemed to be improving — he watched his favorite football team on TV and he was even making Facebook posts and sending us texts.

Then around the third or fourth day, he seemed to be struggling more to breathe. His texts were reduced to merely, "Pray that I can rest and breathe." He couldn't make phone calls because talking was too difficult for him. He stopped posting on social media and we all began to be genuinely concerned. He was still not allowed any visitors, even from his wife or kids. Bobby was extremely social, so such isolation also caused us concern for his emotional state.

Days turned into weeks and he continually got worse. He was transferred to the ICU and put on a ventilator. We continued to pray day and night for him. Bob was a pastor and a missionary to Honduras, so thousands of people were also praying. Then on January 20, his wife and son and daughter were told that there was no more hope. Blood clots had filled his lungs and he could not breathe without the ventilator. The physicians in charge asked his family for permission to remove him from life support.

We were all devastated but still holding out for a miracle. The next day, Lisa received a call to go to the hospital because one of the blood clots had traveled to Bob's heart and he had a massive heart attack. They would permit only her — not his children and grandchildren — to be with him while they removed life support. She had not seen her precious husband for twenty-one days, since the last moments of 2020. Now she was going to be with him only to say goodbye.

Lisa arrived at the hospital at 2:30 p.m. on the twenty-first of January alone and in shock. She held Bobby's head in her hands and gave him one last head rub (his favorite) as he took his final breaths.

I sat at home with my family, weeping from anguish in a depth of my soul that I did not know was possible. I had a picture of Bobby and me when we were young and the ice-cream truck came to our street. He and I would grab our coins and sprint out the front door of our childhood home with great joy and excitement. He usually beat me to the truck.

As I replayed the scene in my mind, he beat me yet again. But this time, when he got to the ice-cream truck it became a beautiful heavenly chariot. I ran toward him as he jumped in the chariot and it rose into the clouds. I was left alone, standing in the street while he flew away to his true home.

It was as if we were kids all over again, and all I wanted to do was to share one last ice cream with him. As he disappeared, I could see myself falling on my knees in front of our driveway, weeping and calling out for him to come back to me — to come back to childhood, to ice cream trucks, to bike rides, to swimming in our pool.

But he was gone. He had finished running and he found home.

Just days later I stood with Lisa, with their kids and grandkids, with Jeff and members of our family, and with many friends on a cold, windy day at a Georgia cemetery as my precious brother's body was placed into the earth next to our parent's graves. I reflected on all the beauty, all the pain, and all the memories that I carried with me about the three people whose bodies were now beneath my feet.

Their souls had found home. I thought how it is us, still here on earth, who are making our way home. I remembered the day that the young teenaged "me" was feeling restless again, so I went to my high school and found the Campus Life group, and for some reason decided to go in. That day, I discovered the door of hope that ushered in salvation in for me, my dad, my mom, and my brother.

Now Bob's family stood there, my family stood with them, and so many who had been touched by what God did for us stood together near us. We had all gone through the same door, leaving the darkness of empty existence and experiencing the joy of looking forward to the brilliant, eternal hope of life with Jesus.

As we walked from the graves that now held the earthly temples of my loved ones, I had to remind myself:

They aren't there any longer.

They gained the hope of eternity and now stood astonished, beholding Jesus, their great reward.

My brother's favorite verse was Jeremiah 29:11: *"For I know the plans I have for you," declares the* LORD, *"plans to prosper you and not to harm you, plans to give you hope and a future."*

Those were the last words he posted on his Facebook page, and they were his final promise fulfilled. He was now standing in the fullness of his hope and eternal future, and is more prosperous than he ever had been! Now, we who are (for now) left here on earth must continue to walk forward, knowing that with every step we are closer to home.

What joy and what hope we have that as we walk through life, we do not journey toward an end — only toward beginnings. We have the promise of the One who loved us before we even knew how desperate and hopeless we were.

Very soon, all who have trusted in the grace by which we have been saved will finally, and completely, find home.

The Door of Hope

At the end of our lives, we arrive at the eternal door that leads every person who has trusted in Jesus as their Savior to their eternal home. There will be no more tears, no more sorrows, no more darkness — and no more wilderness. We will all pass through this final door of hope. On the other side is joy that has always stood before us, beckoning us onward: our Lord Jesus. We leave this world empty-handed, discarding all earthly things, and receive everything the Father has stored up for those who believed in his Son.

No more lack, no more pain, no more loss — everything will be gain. Each door we pass through now leads us closer to the final door of hope, the entrance into fulfillment of every hope and all the dreams of mankind.

Keep walking, keep moving forward, keep hoping; because nothing can take away your eternal hope and reward. Very soon we will thrill to hear "Welcome Home."

Afterword

YOU HAVE JUST READ SOME of my wife's testimony. I know these stories and struggles and victories. Intimately.

And I *still* sat and cried as I was completing the edits on this book. There were no surprises as I read, no turning over forgotten stones in pursuit of the truth, no sudden blinding revelations of "Oh, that's what happened!"

I lived this stuff. I walked with Kathi through the blood and pain and turmoil and darkness — through *the wilderness*. And I wouldn't trade a moment of it. Not because of how much I love her (oh, so much) or because I want you to think I'm some sort of good guy because "I was there" (I'm not that great, trust me) but because Kathi's story is a narrative of life and hope, and the utter, relentless love and mercy and glory of God. It is the story, even though circumstances may differ, of us all.

Kathi's story is the story of our Creator who loves us enough to surround us with his mercy and walk with us through any darkness. The Bible tells us *"Even the darkness is light to you"* and the journey Kathi and I have traveled together has proven that true, in the deepest recesses of our hearts and in our lived experience.

Those of us who have been long in the "prophetic stream" recognize that sometimes there is a glamorizing of cookie-cutter experiences regarding "warfare" and "overcoming." It is easy to discuss these truths in a kind of detached manner, as though the battles we face are "out there" in some nebulous larger arena. Such a viewpoint can become therapeutic — even romanticized — like reading an adventure novel or being caught up in an exciting movie. But the reality is, life is messy and grueling, even brutal, and some of us, despite out best intentions and commitments, have failed spectacularly. We look through church history and see the battlefield littered with catastrophic loss. Such "warfare," when it impacts us up close and personal, is shocking.

The "wilderness" journey is another metaphor that we can be tempted to pass over lightly. Experience a season of difficulty or disappointment, and we opine sorrowfully about wandering forty years like Israel. Or we smile dutifully and try to bolster our spirits by glibly stating "I'm trusting the Lord!" even though everything inside screams with questions. A real wilderness is a hard place, frightening and dangerous. In the wilderness, none of our traditional comforts or safe spaces are available, so we tremble and wonder why all the promises of God have vanished like morning mist.

But God often sends his servants into the wilderness. The Son of God himself was led there by the Holy Spirit. The seeking child of God who presses in to know him will, at some point, find himself or herself wandering, lonely, tired, discouraged, hungry, and thirsty. It is disheartening to discover the compass you've depended on doesn't point toward home; spin the needle as you may, you just find it directing you deeper into the wasteland.

However, if in the emptiness we will gather our spiritual wits about us and be still, quieting our propensity toward unbelief and turning toward the breath of the Spirit, we can hear voices dancing lightly on his wind, carried from messengers past who cried out in the arid wilderness, "Make straight the ways of the Lord."

Kathi is one of those voices. She tells her story straight. She tells her story raw. She tells her story real — not hiding the dark parts, not glossing over the failure, not pretending to be someone she is not.

My wife has offered us her "genuine self." And in the offering, her story breathes life as she sings of how anguish and defeat led to beauty and triumph. She encountered the power of mercy and tenderness granted from the heart and hand of an always good, ever faithful, infinitely loving Father who led her to her heart's true home.

God is merciful. God is kind. God is good.

And his love is everlasting, beyond all we can hope or think.

I pray that reading this has shown you that he will rescue anyone who looks to him with the simple hope that he will help you find your way. Kathi's story serves as a signpost directing you to a path leading to warmth and safety that awaits as you walk with the One who loves you and will lead you gently into life.

Into your true home.

—Jeffrey Pelton

Resources for Healing

ARK77 RECOVERY CENTER TREATMENT HELPS adults with all types of mental health issues. Our clinical team explores carefully with our residents the source of their struggles. Families are highly encouraged to participate in resident's treatment. We treat eating disorders, anxiety, depression, PTSD, and trauma. We educate our residents, so they are able to restart their new recovered life after transformation at Ark77 Recovery Center. There is hope in the work we do.

Ark77 Recovery Center
91804 Mill Creek Road, Rainbow, OR 97413
United States
Kail Harbick (541) 915-8007
https://ark77.com/

Additional ed information

If you, or someone you care about, has an eating disorder, the following are some websites offering resources including a confidential self-test, resources for finding facilities, free hotline numbers, and online support groups.

These sites are not meant to be used for comprehensive medical advice or treatment, but they can help you begin your journey to healing.

+ https://cedcn.org/
+ https://eatingdisorders.com/test/eating-disorder-self-test
+ https://www.eatingsdisorders.com/christian-based-eating-disorder-treatment

Suicide prevention

Visit Cru (Campus Crusade for Christ International)

+ https://www.cru.org/us/en/train-and-grow/life-and-relationships/hardships/suicide-prevention-resources.html

National Suicide Prevention Hotline

+ Call 1-800-273-TALK (1-800-273-8255)
+ Use the online Lifeline Crisis Chat (https://suicidepreventionlifeline.org/chat/)

Download a handout on suicide prevention from Action Alliance here:

+ https://theactionalliance.org/sites/default/files/action_alliance_marketing_handout_2.pdf

Faces of Dreams International

Faces of Dreams International pursues opportunities to help provide for the real needs of impoverished people around the globe who have been victimized by natural disaster, famine, pandemic, or lack of proper education.

When people lose hope, they become desperate. Our projects provide hope as they alleviate concerns about housing, lack of education, and food insecurity.

https://facesofdreamsinternational.com/

Faces of Dreams YouTube videos

https://youtu.be/6nNWMAW0Bc4
https://youtu.be/DrrxDeeFw7U
https://youtu.be/qPF7EMFF1eg

To Bobby: We will not let go of your dreams for Honduras or Faces of Dreams International. We all miss you so much and we will continue to love what you loved and who you loved. —Kathi

Pastor Bob Cheli was our beloved friend and very influential in the founding of Faces of Dreams International. It was our shared vision, and he was set to be the first Executive Director of the organization before his passing. It seemed to be a dream coming true for him, so we plan to keep his dream alive! His fingerprints, footprints, and influence will always be felt, and shown, in how we operate. His devotion, dreams, and inspiration lives on in the lives he touched in Honduras, with the people he introduced to Faces of Dreams, and with our family and staff here, as well as Ministerio Faces of Dreams in Honduras. The dreams that he shared with us, the logo that he designed, and legacy that he left behind will not be forgotten.

To Bob, it was our honor to have you with us, and we will see you again. Keep watching over us as we stay in the fight! Your dreams and vision are currently still coming to pass. They will live on in us, your beautiful family, and in Honduras. God's got this! —Pastor Mike Patton

Works Cited

Bolton, Martha. "Martha Bolton Quotes," accessed 9/29/21. https://www.azquotes.com/author/52673-Martha_Bolton.

Brooks, Victoria. *Ministering to God: The Reach of the Heart*. Cedar Rapids, IA: Arrow Publications, 1995.

Buckingham, Jamie. *A Way Through the Wilderness*. Grand Rapids, MI: Chosen Books, 1983.

Eldredge, Staci. *Defiant Joy: Taking Hold of Hope, Beauty, and Life in a Hurting World*. Nashville, TN: Nelson Books, 2018.

Foster, Richard J. "Seeking the Kingdom Quotes," Goodreads. https://www.goodreads.com/work/quotes/250461-seeking-the-kingdom-devotions-for-the-daily-journey-of-faith

Gire, Ken. *Windows of the Soul: Experiencing God in New Ways*. Grand Rapids, MI: Zondervan, 1996.

Graves, Marlena. *A Beautiful Disaster: Finding Hope in the Midst of Brokenness*. Grand Rapids, MI: Brazos Press, 2014.

Keller, Phillip. *A Shepherd Looks at Psalm 23*. Grand Rapids, MI: Zondervan, 1970.

Key Word Study Bible. Chattanooga, TN: AMG Publishers, 2015.

Lewis, C. S. *The Chronicles of Narnia: The Signature Edition.*
NY: HarperCollins, 2015.

Shaw Luci. *The Crime of Living Cautiously: Hearing God's
Call to Adventure.* Downers Grove, IL: InterVarsity
Press, 2005.

About the Author

KATHI PELTON is an author and prophetic voice to the church. She and her husband Jeffrey walk with nations and individuals to see God's original intent fulfilled on the earth, and she has spent years helping people encounter the healing love and mercy of God. Her passion is to see the establishment of genuine family gathered in the unity expressed by Jesus's prayer in John 17.

Kathi and Jeffrey married in 1983 and together have raised four children. They currently have three grandchildren, and are filled with eager expectations of many more!

The Peltons live in the Portland, Oregon region and attend Father's House City Ministries, where they serve as part of the leadership team.

CPSIA information can be obtained
at www.ICGtesting.com
Printed in the USA
FSHW012348171121
86238FS

9 781951 611286